Soul
The Chord Songbook

Wise Publications
London/New York/Paris/Sydney/Copenhagen/Madrid/Tokyo

Exclusive Distributors:

Music Sales Limited
8/9 Frith Street,
London W1D 3JB, England.
Music Sales Pty Limited
120 Rothschild Avenue,
Rosebery, NSW 2018, Australia.

Order No. AM966108
ISBN 0-7119-8370-4
This book © Copyright 2000 by Wise Publications

> This publication is not authorised for sale in
> the United States of America and/or Canada.

Unauthorised reproduction of any part of this publication by any
means including photocopying is an infringement of copyright.

Compiled by Nick Crispin
Music arranged by Rob Smith
Music engraved by The Pitts

Cover photograph courtesy of Redferns

Printed in the United Kingdom by
Caligraving Limited, Thetford, Nolfolk.

Your Guarantee of Quality
As publishers, we strive to produce every book
to the highest commercial standards.
This book has been carefully designed to minimise awkward
page turns and to make playing from it a real pleasure.
Particular care has been given to specifying acid-free,
neutral-sized paper made from pulps which have not been
elemental chlorine bleached. This pulp is from farmed sustainable
forests and was produced with special regard for the environment.
Throughout, the printing and binding have been planned to
ensure a sturdy, attractive publication which should give years
of enjoyment. If your copy fails to meet our high standards,
please inform us and we will gladly replace it.

Music Sales' complete catalogue describes thousands
of titles and is available in full colour sections by subject,
direct from Music Sales Limited. Please state your areas of interest
and send a cheque/postal order for £1.50 for postage to:
Music Sales Limited, Newmarket Road,
Bury St. Edmunds, Suffolk IP33 3YB.

www.musicsales.com

Band Of Gold 4
Dance To The Music 6
Go Now 8
I Get The Sweetest Feeling 12
I Got You (I Feel Good) 10
I Heard It Through The Grapevine 15
I Say A Little Prayer 26
I Wish 18
I'd Rather Go Blind 20
In The Midnight Hour 22
Midnight Train To Georgia 24
Rescue Me 29
Stay With Me Baby 32
Summer Breeze 34
(Take A Little) Piece Of My Heart 36
Take Me To The River 38
Try A Little Tenderness 40
Under The Boardwalk 42
What'd I Say 44
Why Can't We Live Together 46

Playing Guide: Relative Tuning/Reading Chord Boxes 48

Band Of Gold

Words & Music by
Ronald Dunbar & Edith Wayne

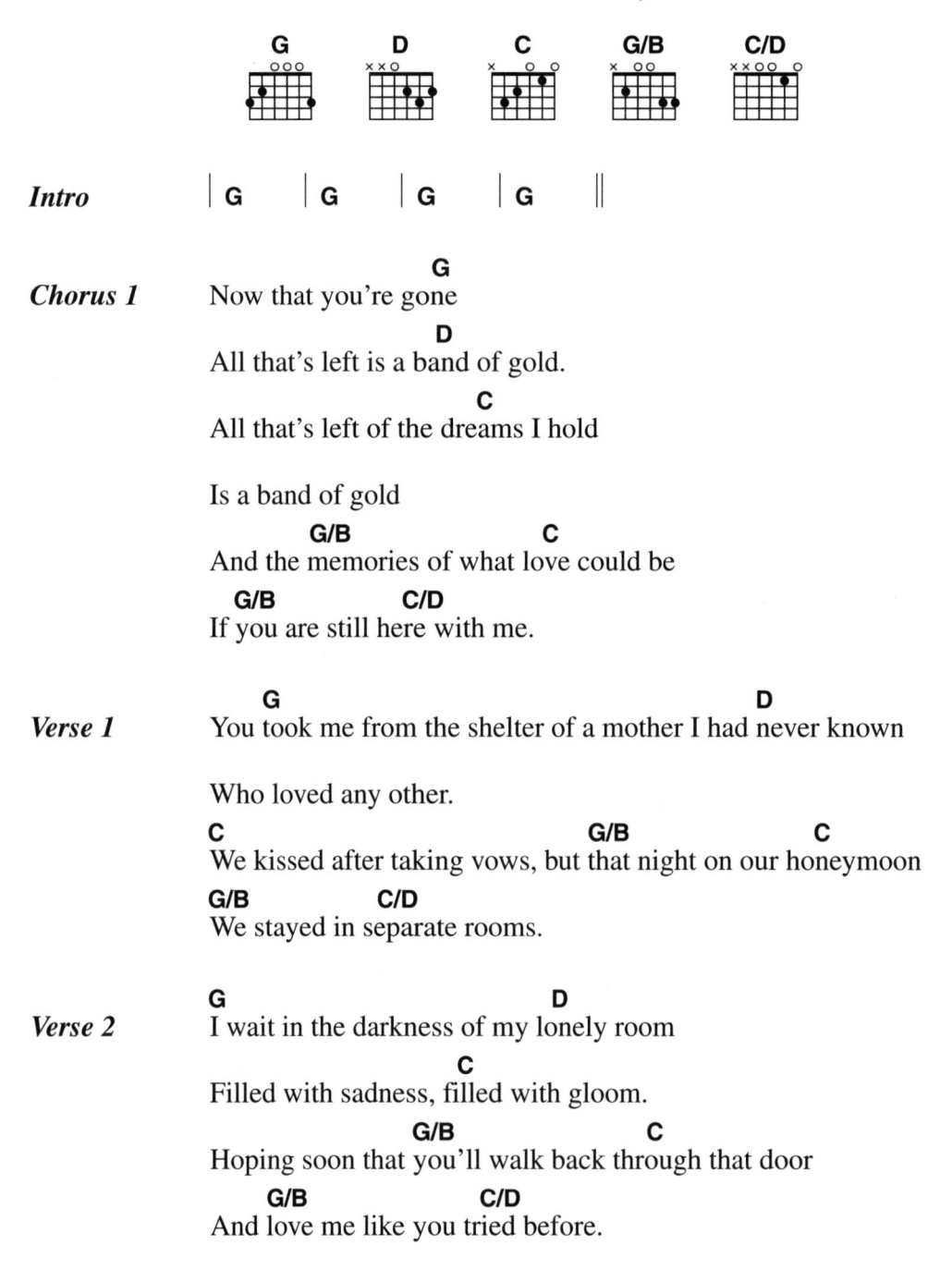

G   D   C   G/B   C/D

Intro | G | G | G | G ||

Chorus 1
                    G
Now that you're gone
                           D
All that's left is a band of gold.
                           C
All that's left of the dreams I hold

Is a band of gold
         G/B   C
And the memories of what love could be
   G/B   C/D
If you are still here with me.

Verse 1
           G   D
You took me from the shelter of a mother I had never known

Who loved any other.
 C   G/B   C
We kissed after taking vows, but that night on our honeymoon
 G/B   C/D
We stayed in separate rooms.

Verse 2
         G   D
I wait in the darkness of my lonely room
                   C
Filled with sadness, filled with gloom.
             G/B   C
Hoping soon that you'll walk back through that door
  G/B   C/D
And love me like you tried before.

© Copyright 1970 Gold Forever Music Incorporated, USA.
Universal/MCA Music Limited, 77 Fulham Palace Road, London W6.
All Rights Reserved. International Copyright Secured.

Chorus 2

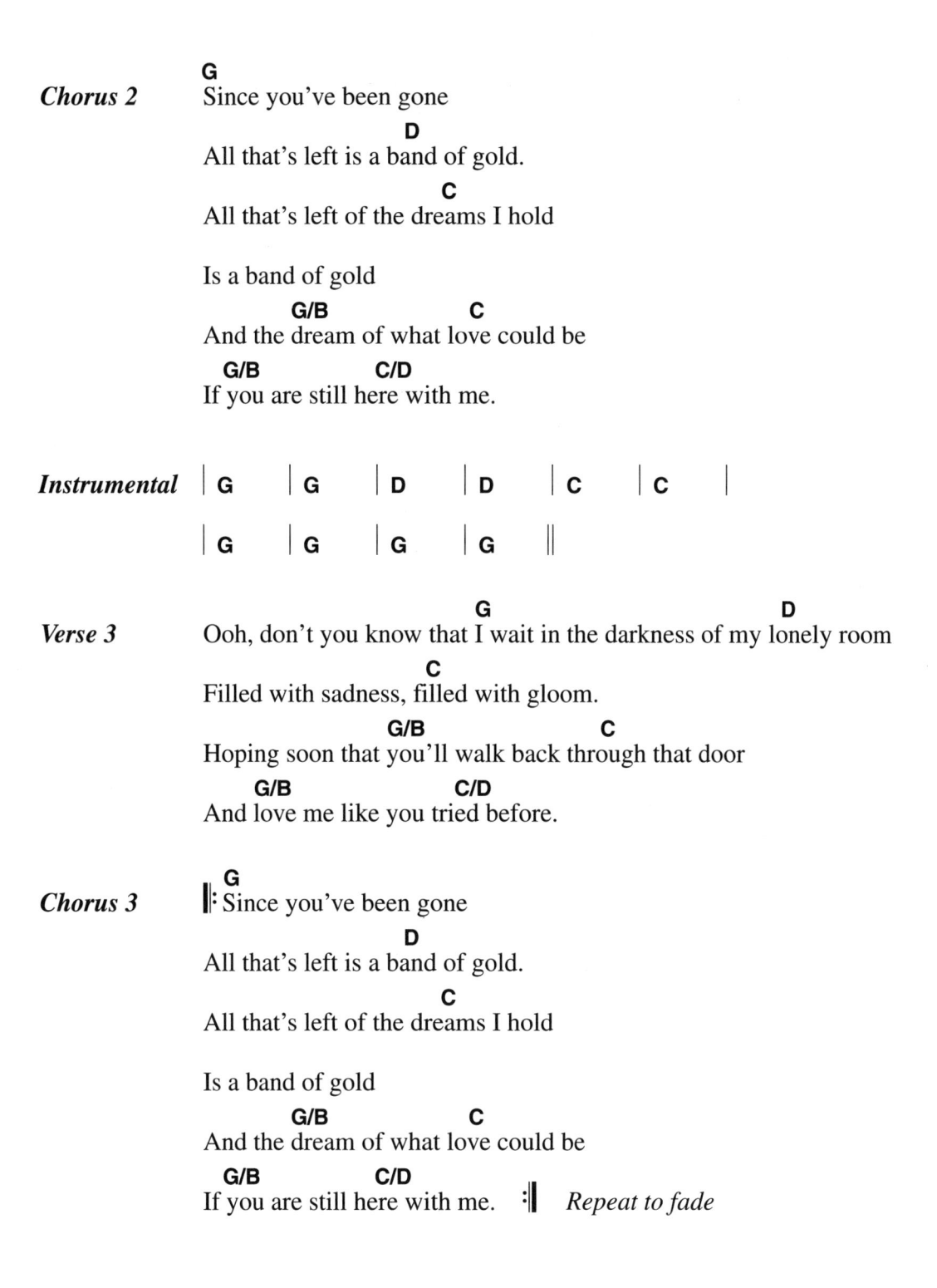

    G
Since you've been gone
                D
All that's left is a band of gold.
                  C
All that's left of the dreams I hold

Is a band of gold
        G/B   **C**
And the dream of what love could be
      G/B   **C/D**
If you are still here with me.

Instrumental | G | G | D | D | C | C |

                    | G | G | G | G ||

Verse 3

                        G   **D**
Ooh, don't you know that I wait in the darkness of my lonely room
                   C
Filled with sadness, filled with gloom.
                 G/B   **C**
Hoping soon that you'll walk back through that door
         G/B   **C/D**
And love me like you tried before.

Chorus 3

      G
||: Since you've been gone
                D
All that's left is a band of gold.
                  C
All that's left of the dreams I hold

Is a band of gold
        G/B   **C**
And the dream of what love could be
      G/B   **C/D**
If you are still here with me. :|| *Repeat to fade*

Dance To The Music

Words & Music by
Sylvester Stewart

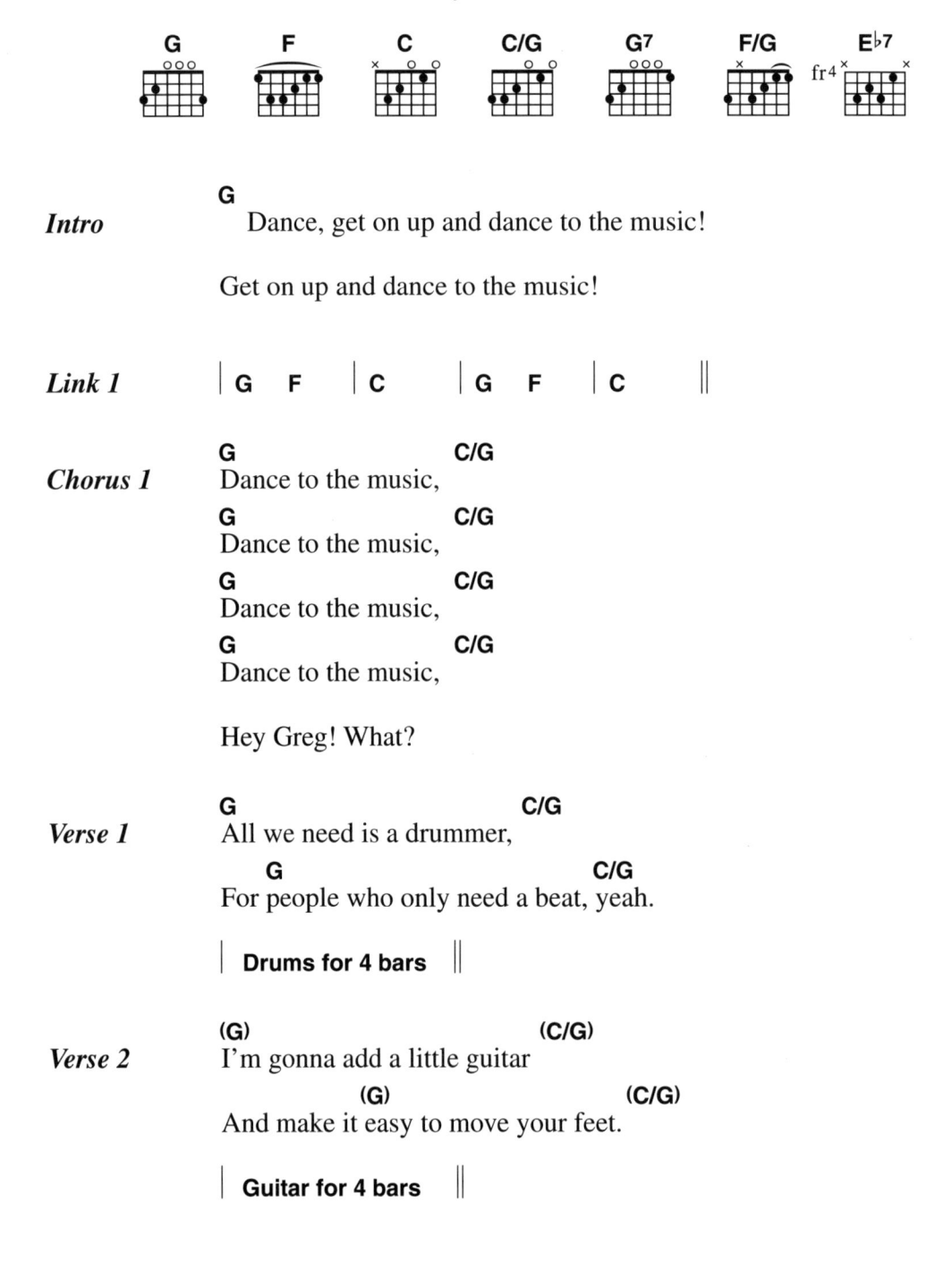

G F C C/G G7 F/G E♭7

Intro
      G
Dance, get on up and dance to the music!

Get on up and dance to the music!

Link 1
| G F | C | G F | C ||

Chorus 1
G   C/G
Dance to the music,
G   C/G
Dance to the music,
G   C/G
Dance to the music,
G   C/G
Dance to the music,

Hey Greg! What?

Verse 1
G   C/G
All we need is a drummer,
     G   C/G
For people who only need a beat, yeah.

| **Drums for 4 bars** ||

Verse 2
(G)   (C/G)
I'm gonna add a little guitar
        (G)   (C/G)
And make it easy to move your feet.

| **Guitar for 4 bars** ||

© Copyright 1968 Daly City Music, USA.
Carlin Music Corporation, Iron Bridge House, 3 Bridge Approach, London NW1.
All Rights Reserved. International Copyright Secured.

Verse 3

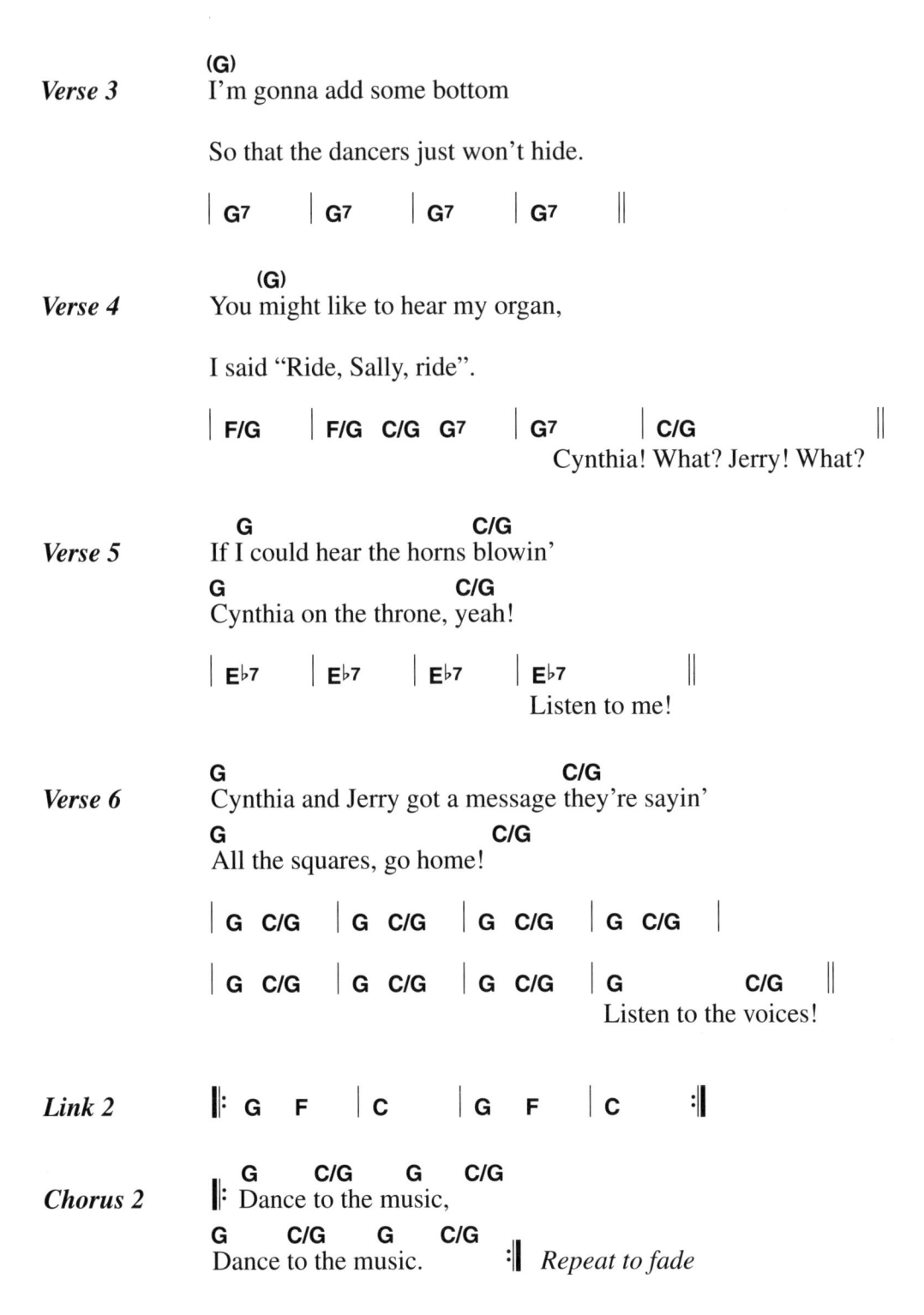

    (G)
I'm gonna add some bottom

So that the dancers just won't hide.

| **G7** | **G7** | **G7** | **G7** ||

Verse 4

    (G)
You might like to hear my organ,

I said "Ride, Sally, ride".

| **F/G** | **F/G   C/G   G7** | **G7** | **C/G** ||
                                             Cynthia! What? Jerry! What?

Verse 5

   G   **C/G**
If I could hear the horns blowin'
G   **C/G**
Cynthia on the throne, yeah!

| **E♭7** | **E♭7** | **E♭7** | **E♭7** ||
                                Listen to me!

Verse 6

 G   **C/G**
Cynthia and Jerry got a message they're sayin'
G   **C/G**
All the squares, go home!

| **G   C/G** | **G   C/G** | **G   C/G** | **G   C/G** |

| **G   C/G** | **G   C/G** | **G   C/G** | **G   C/G** ||
                                             Listen to the voices!

Link 2

‖: **G   F** | **C** | **G   F** | **C** :‖

Chorus 2

  G   **C/G**   **G**   **C/G**
‖: Dance to the music,
G   **C/G**   **G**   **C/G**
Dance to the music.   :‖ *Repeat to fade*

Go Now

Words & Music by
Larry Banks & Milton Bennett

[Chord diagrams: G, G/F#, G/E, G/D, C, Am, D, D#m, Em, Bm, C/D]

Capo first fret

Intro
    NC.
We've already said

| G | G/F# | G/E | G/D | C | Am |

Goodbye,

  D
And since you gotta go,

Oh you had better:

Chorus 1
  G   G/F#
Go now,

  G/E   G/D   C   Am
Go now, go now, go now,

  D   D#m Em
Before you'll see me cry. _____

Verse 1
And I don't want you to tell me
Bm
    Just what you intend to do now,
Em
    'Cause how many times do I have to tell you

Darlin', darlin', darlin', darlin', darlin',
Bm   **Am**   **D**
    I'm still in love, still in love with you now.

© Copyright 1963 Trio Music Company Incorporated, USA.
Carlin Music Corporation, Iron Bridge House, 3 Bridge Approach, London NW1
for the British Commonwealth (excluding Canada and Australasia),
the Republic of Ireland and Israel.
All Rights Reserved. International Copyright Secured.

Link

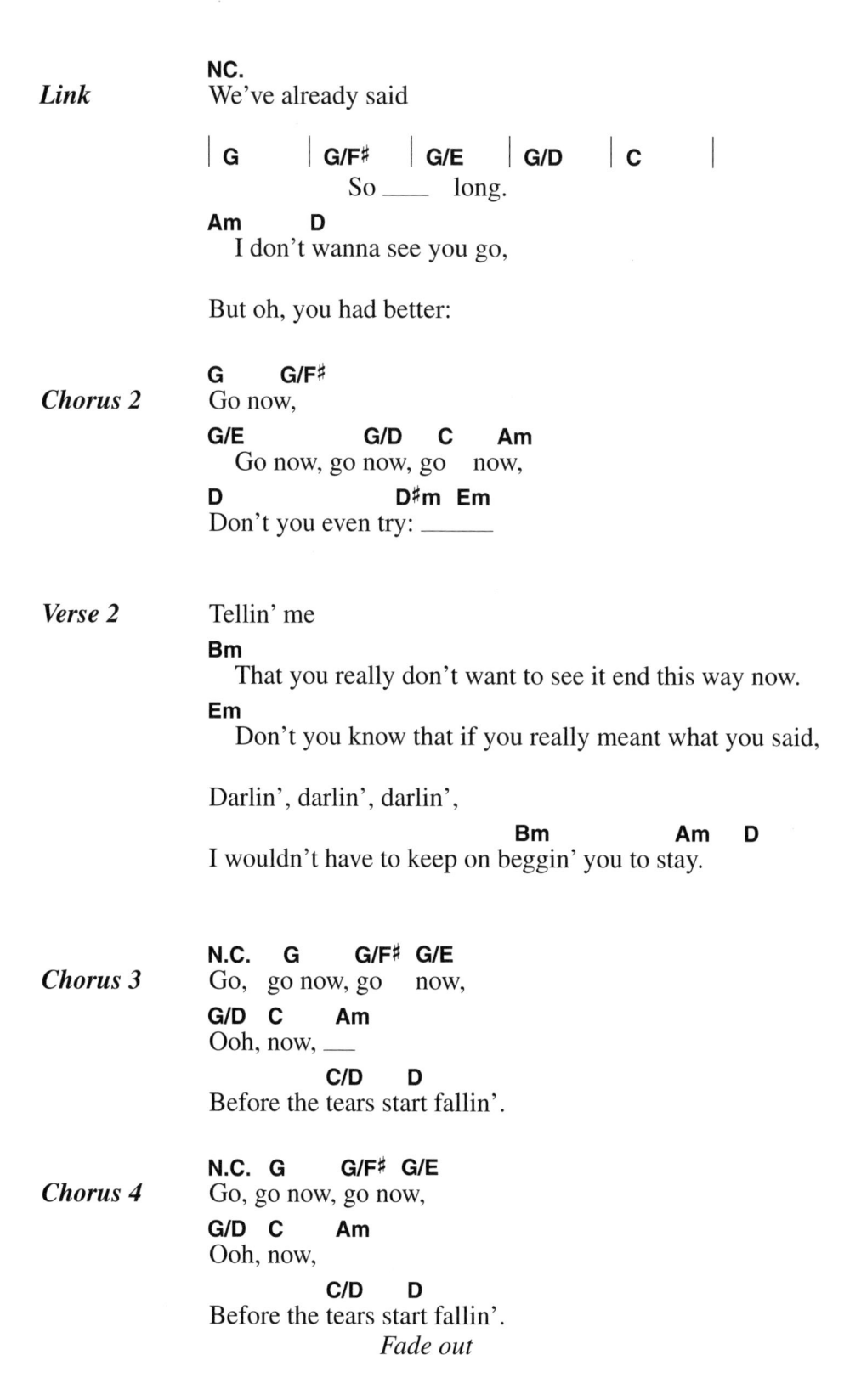

NC.
We've already said

| **G** | **G/F♯** | **G/E** | **G/D** | **C** |

So ___ long.

Am **D**
  I don't wanna see you go,

But oh, you had better:

Chorus 2

G **G/F♯**
Go now,

G/E **G/D C Am**
  Go now, go now, go now,

D **D♯m Em**
Don't you even try: ___

Verse 2

Tellin' me

Bm
  That you really don't want to see it end this way now.

Em
  Don't you know that if you really meant what you said,

Darlin', darlin', darlin',

              Bm **Am D**
I wouldn't have to keep on beggin' you to stay.

Chorus 3

N.C. G **G/F♯ G/E**
Go, go now, go now,

G/D C **Am**
Ooh, now, ___

       C/D **D**
Before the tears start fallin'.

Chorus 4

N.C. G **G/F♯ G/E**
Go, go now, go now,

G/D C **Am**
Ooh, now,

       C/D **D**
Before the tears start fallin'.
                Fade out

I Got You (I Feel Good)

Words & Music by
James Brown

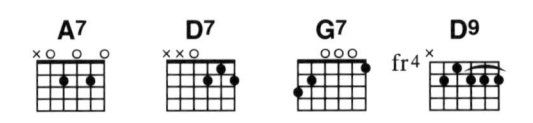

A7   D7   G7   D9

Verse 1

    (A7)   D7
Whoa! I feel good, I knew that I would, now,
      G7   D7
I feel good, I knew that I would, now.
     A7   G7   D9
So good, so good, I got you.

Verse 2

                D7
Whoa! I feel nice, like sugar and spice,
     G7   D7
I feel nice, like sugar and spice,
    A7   G7   D9
So nice, so nice, 'cause I got you.

Link 1

| (D7) | (D7) | (D7) | (D7) ||

Middle 1

       G7
When I hold you in my arms
D7
  I know I can do no wrong, now.
      G7
When I hold you in my arms
     A7
My love can't do me no harm.

Verse 3

            D7
And I feel nice, like sugar and spice,
     G7   D7
I feel nice, like sugar and spice,
    A7   G7   D9
So nice, so nice, I got you.

© Copyright 1966 Fort Knox Music Company Incorporated, USA.
Lark Music Limited (Carlin), Iron Bridge House, 3 Bridge Approach, London NW1.
All Rights Reserved. International Copyright Secured.

Link 2 | (D7) | (D7) | (D7) | (D7)   ‖

Middle 2
          G7
When I hold you in my arms
 D7
I know that I can't do no wrong.
       G7
And when I hold you in my arms
  A7
My love can't do me no harm.

Verse 4
          D7
And I feel nice, like sugar and spice,
     G7   **D7**
I feel nice, like sugar and spice,
 A7   **G7**   **D9**
So nice, so nice, well I got you.

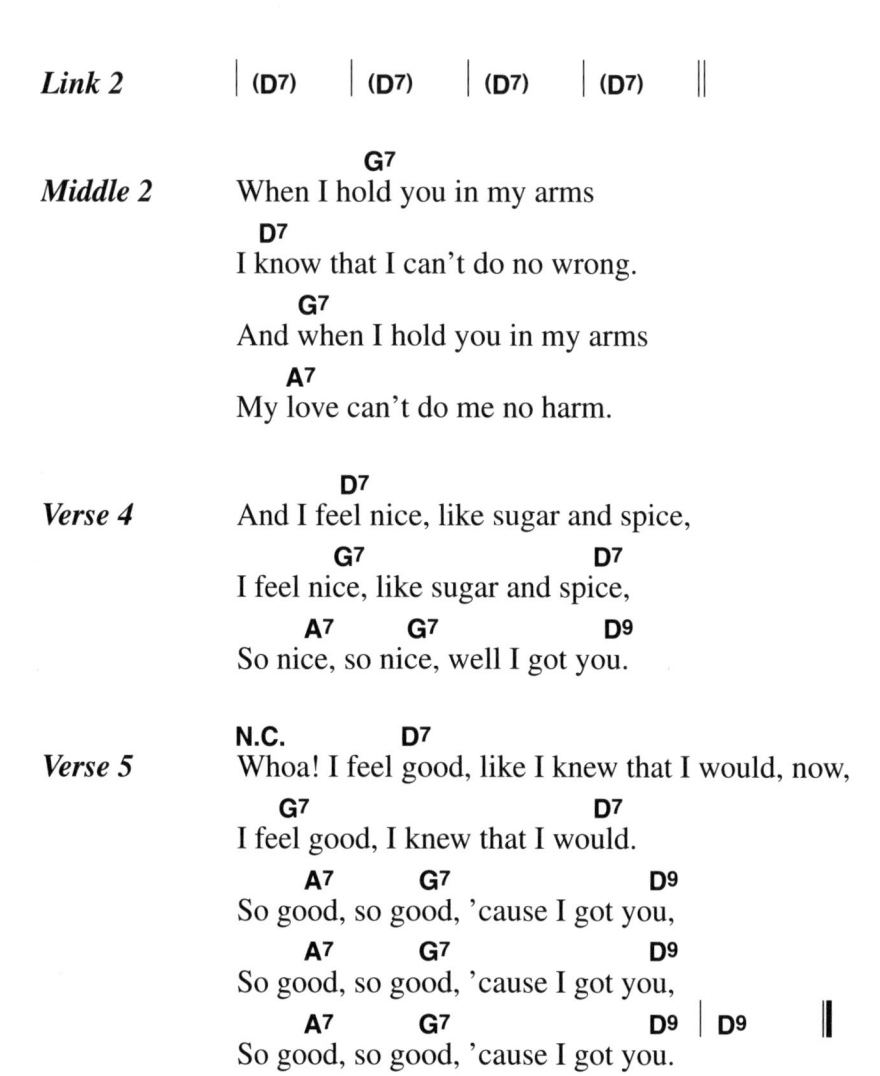

Verse 5
N.C.   **D7**
Whoa! I feel good, like I knew that I would, now,
 G7   **D7**
I feel good, I knew that I would.
  A7   **G7**   **D9**
So good, so good, 'cause I got you,
  A7   **G7**   **D9**
So good, so good, 'cause I got you,
  A7   **G7**   **D9** | **D9**   ‖
So good, so good, 'cause I got you.

I Get The Sweetest Feeling

Words & Music by
Van McCoy & Alicia Evelyn

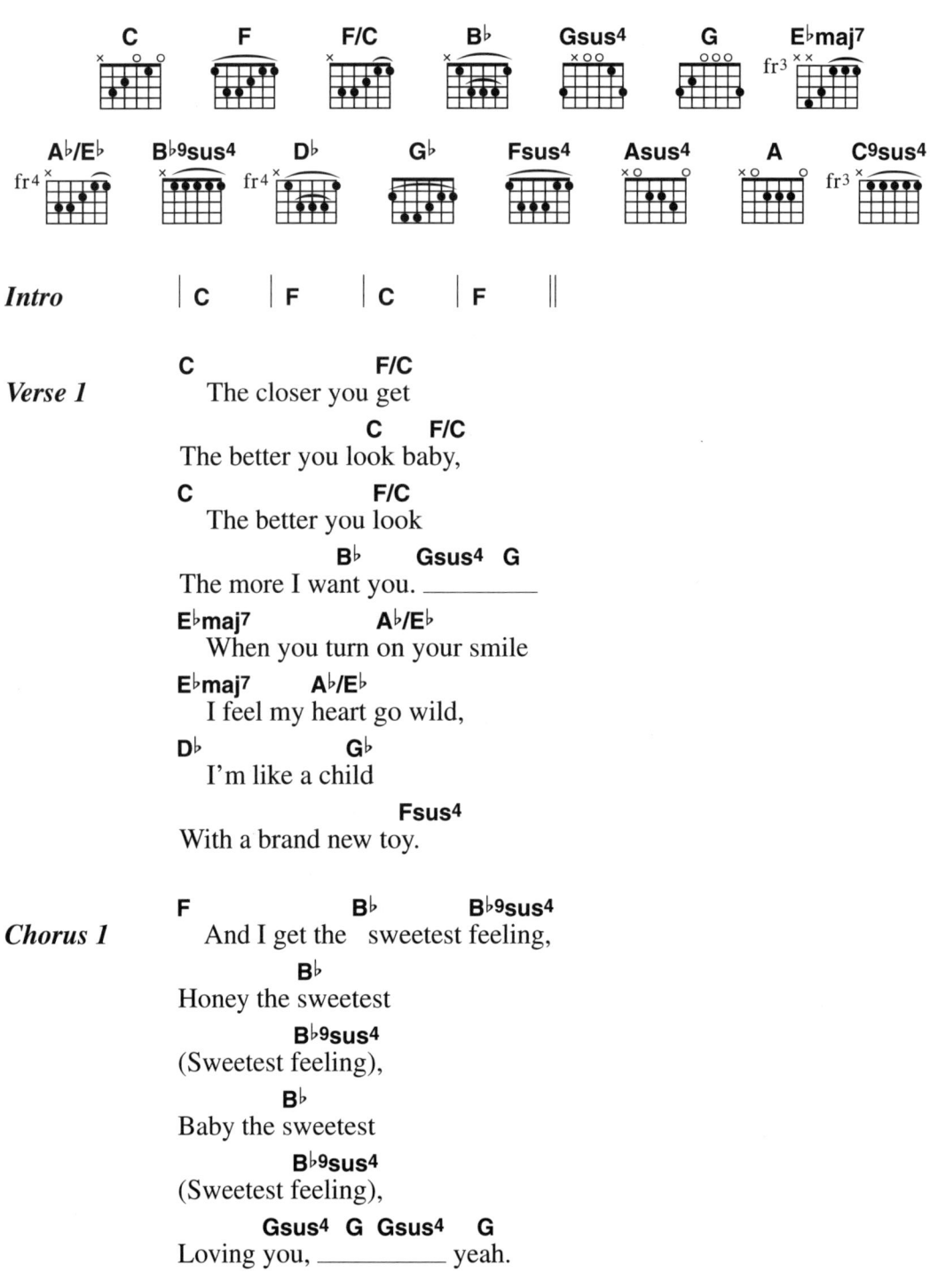

Intro | C | F | C | F ||

Verse 1
      C   F/C
The closer you get
               C   F/C
The better you look baby,
    C   F/C
The better you look
             B♭   Gsus4 G
The more I want you. _____
E♭maj7   A♭/E♭
When you turn on your smile
E♭maj7   A♭/E♭
I feel my heart go wild,
D♭   G♭
I'm like a child
                Fsus4
With a brand new toy.

Chorus 1
   F   B♭   B♭9sus4
And I get the sweetest feeling,
  B♭
Honey the sweetest
  B♭9sus4
(Sweetest feeling),
  B♭
Baby the sweetest
  B♭9sus4
(Sweetest feeling),
  Gsus4 G Gsus4   G
Loving you, _____ yeah.

© Copyright 1968 (renewed) Alley Music Corporation, USA.
Carlin Music Corporation, Iron Bridge House, 3 Bridge Approach, London NW1
for the British Commonwealth (excluding Canada and Australasia),
Hong Kong, the Republic of Ireland and Israel.
All Rights Reserved. International Copyright Secured.

Verse 2

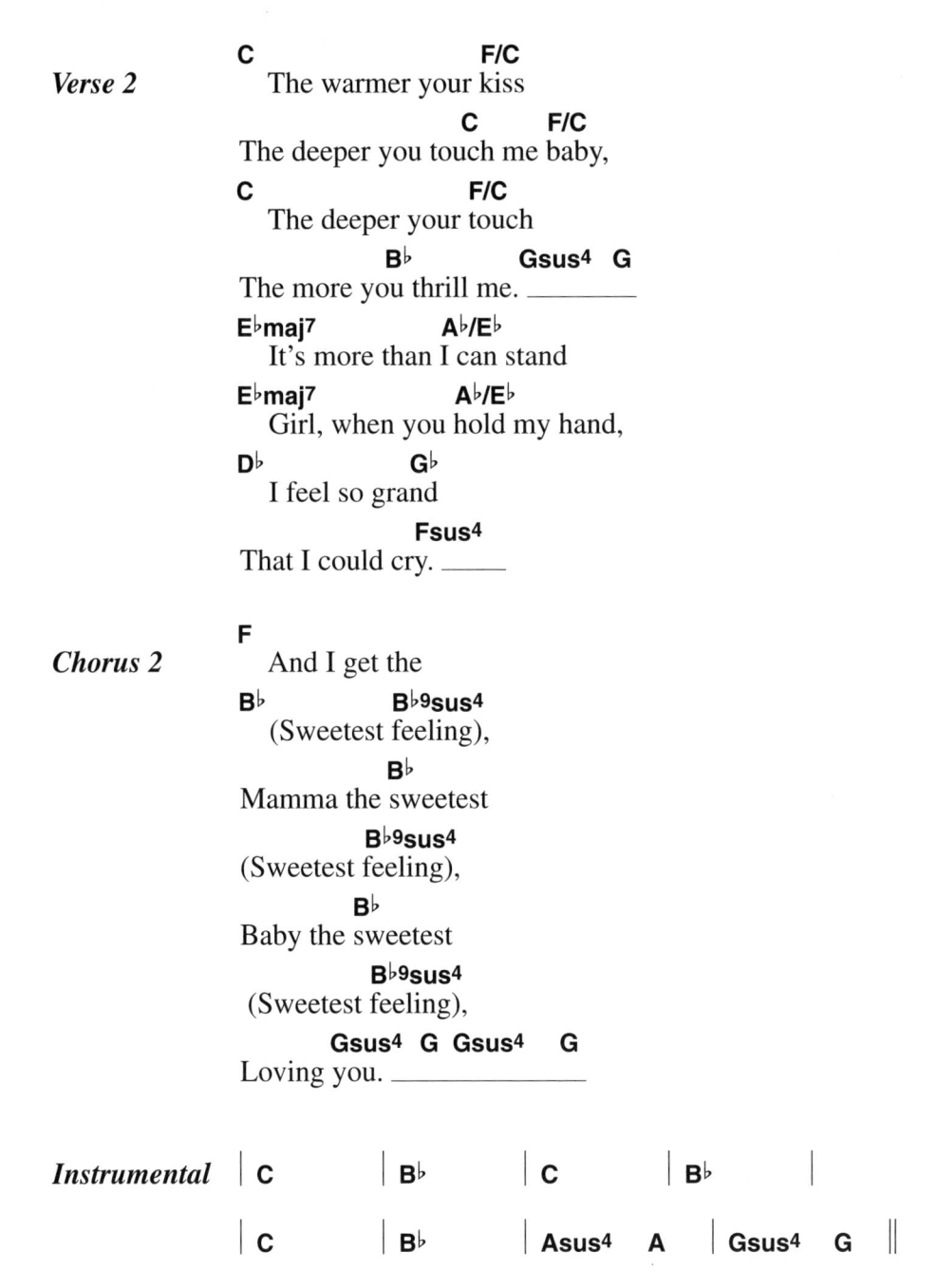

    C   F/C
    The warmer your kiss
          C   F/C
   The deeper you touch me baby,
  C   F/C
    The deeper your touch
         B♭   Gsus⁴ G
    The more you thrill me. _____
  E♭maj⁷   A♭/E♭
    It's more than I can stand
  E♭maj⁷   A♭/E♭
    Girl, when you hold my hand,
  D♭   G♭
    I feel so grand
         Fsus⁴
  That I could cry. _____

Chorus 2

    F
     And I get the
  B♭   B♭9sus⁴
   (Sweetest feeling),
        B♭
  Mamma the sweetest
       B♭9sus⁴
  (Sweetest feeling),
       B♭
  Baby the sweetest
       B♭9sus⁴
  (Sweetest feeling),
     Gsus⁴ G Gsus⁴ G
  Loving you. _____

Instrumental | C | B♭ | C | B♭ |

        | C | B♭ | Asus⁴ A | Gsus⁴ G ||

Verse 3

     C   **F/C**
  Ooh, the greater your love
         C   **F/C**
  The stronger you hold me baby,
C   **F/C**
  The stronger your hold
       B♭ **Gsus⁴** **G**
  The more I need you. _____
E♭maj7   **A♭/E♭**
  With every passing day
E♭maj7   **A♭/E♭**
  I love you more in every way,
D♭   **G♭**
  I'm in love to stay
        Fsus⁴
  And I wanna say:

Chorus 3

  F
  I get the
B♭   **B♭9sus⁴**
  (Sweetest feeling),
     B♭
  Baby the sweetest
      B♭9sus⁴
  (Sweetest feeling),
      B♭
  Honey the sweetest
      B♭9sus⁴
  (Sweetest feeling),
    Gsus⁴ **G** **Gsus⁴** **G**
  Loving you. _____

Outro

    C   **C9sus⁴**
  Ah, (sweetest feeling),
      C
  Baby the sweetest
      C9sus⁴
  (Sweetest feeling),
     C
  Sweetest, sweetest
      C9sus⁴
  (Sweetest feeling). *Fade out*

I Heard It Through The Grapevine

Words & Music by
Norman Whitfield & Barrett Strong

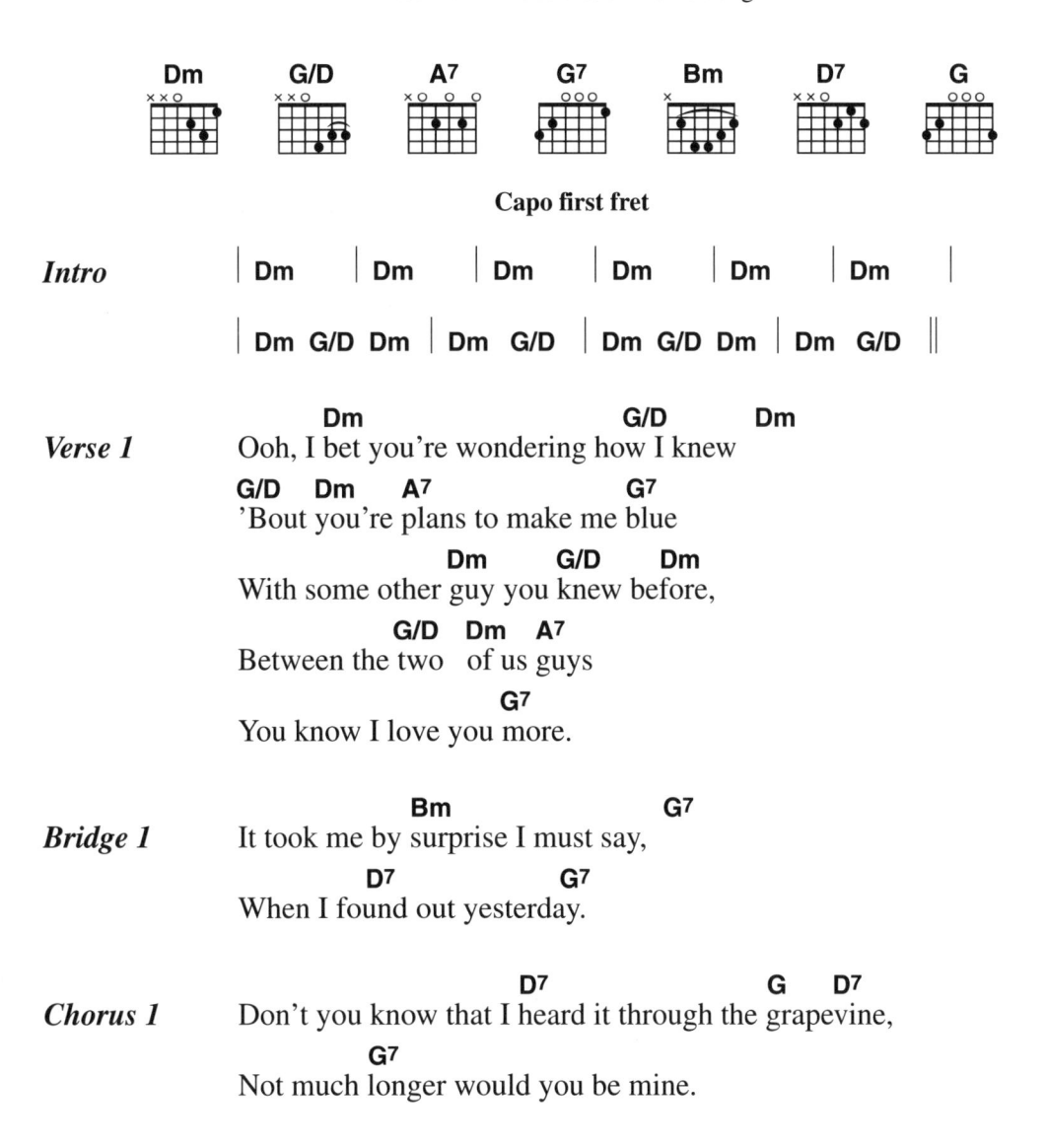

Dm   G/D   A7   G7   Bm   D7   G

Capo first fret

Intro | Dm | Dm | Dm | Dm | Dm | Dm |
| Dm G/D Dm | Dm G/D | Dm G/D Dm | Dm G/D ||

Verse 1
       Dm   G/D   Dm
Ooh, I bet you're wondering how I knew
G/D   Dm   A7   G7
'Bout you're plans to make me blue
        Dm   G/D   Dm
With some other guy you knew before,
           G/D   Dm   A7
Between the two   of us guys
            G7
You know I love you more.

Bridge 1
            Bm   G7
It took me by surprise I must say,
      D7   G7
When I found out yesterday.

Chorus 1
            D7   G   D7
Don't you know that I heard it through the grapevine,
    G7
Not much longer would you be mine.

© Copyright 1966 Stone Agate Music/Jobete Music Company Incorporated, USA.
Jobete Music (UK) Limited/EMI Music Publishing Limited, 127 Charing Cross Road, London WC2
for the United Kingdom and the Republic of Ireland.
All Rights Reserved. International Copyright Secured.

cont.

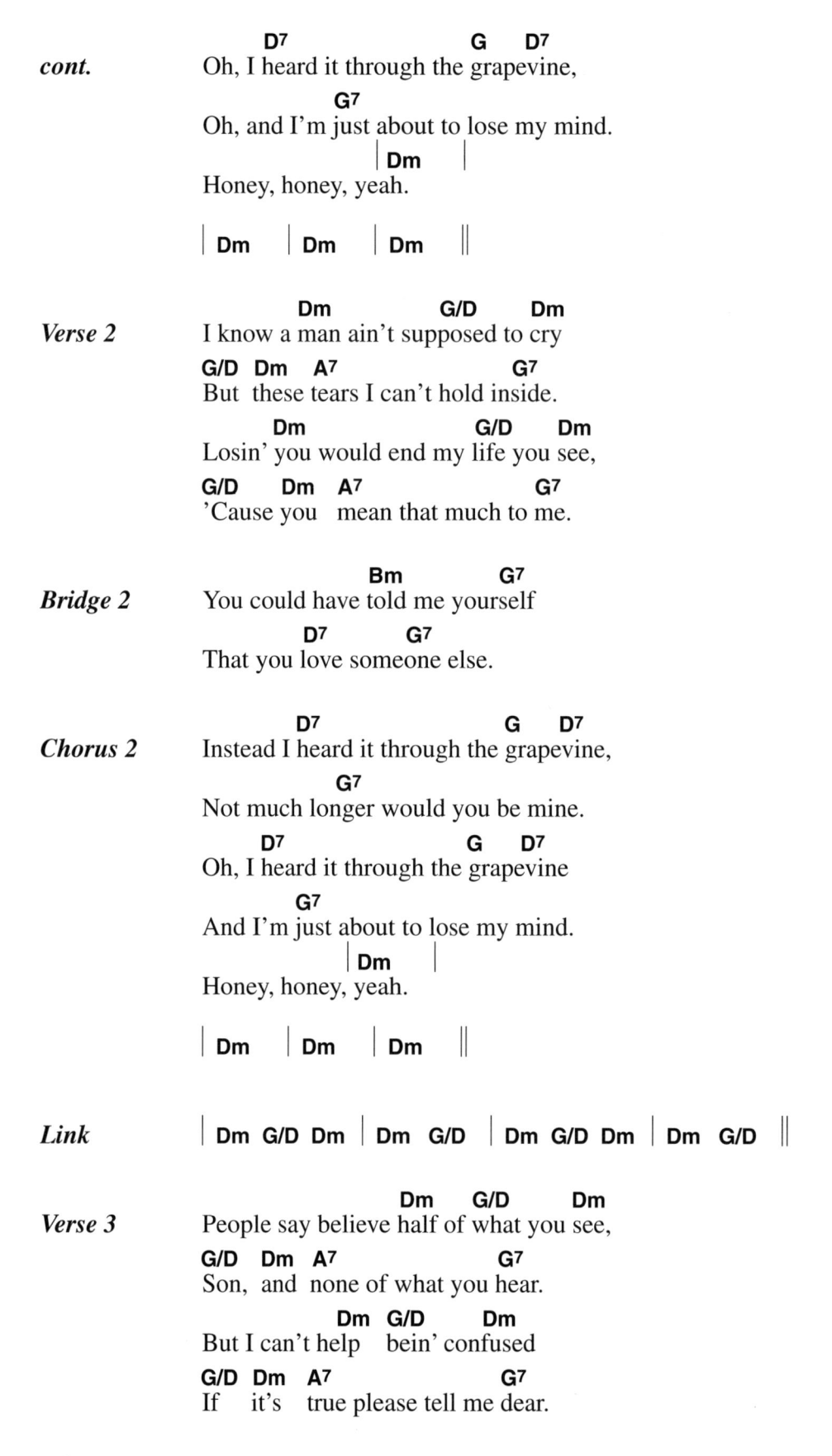

        D7   G   D7
Oh, I heard it through the grapevine,
              G7
Oh, and I'm just about to lose my mind.
                   | Dm |
Honey, honey, yeah.

| Dm | Dm | Dm ||

Verse 2

         Dm   G/D   Dm
I know a man ain't supposed to cry
G/D Dm   A7   G7
But these tears I can't hold inside.
        Dm   G/D   Dm
Losin' you would end my life you see,
G/D   Dm   A7   G7
'Cause you   mean that much to me.

Bridge 2

                Bm   G7
You could have told me yourself
          D7   G7
That you love someone else.

Chorus 2

         D7   G   D7
Instead I heard it through the grapevine,
            G7
Not much longer would you be mine.
     D7   G   D7
Oh, I heard it through the grapevine
        G7
And I'm just about to lose my mind.
               | Dm |
Honey, honey, yeah.

| Dm | Dm | Dm ||

Link

| Dm G/D Dm | Dm G/D | Dm G/D Dm | Dm G/D ||

Verse 3

                      Dm   G/D   Dm
People say believe half of what you see,
G/D Dm A7   G7
Son, and none of what you hear.
                Dm G/D   Dm
But I can't help   bein' confused
G/D Dm   A7   G7
If   it's   true please tell me dear.

Bridge 3

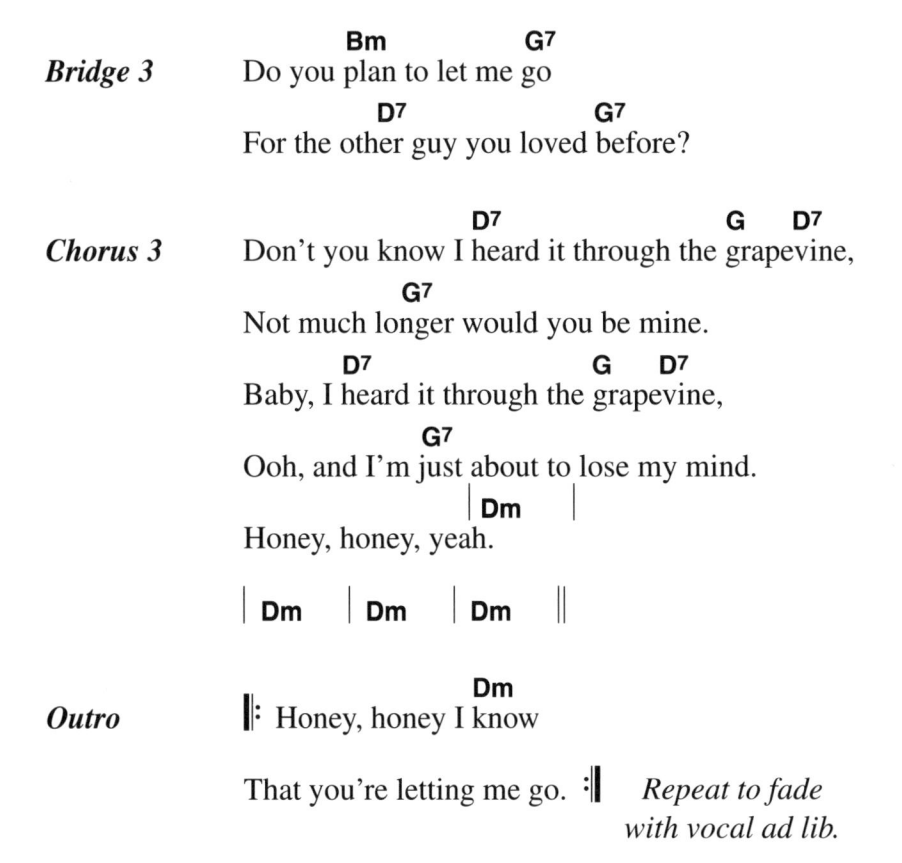

           Bm   **G7**
Do you plan to let me go
      D7   **G7**
For the other guy you loved before?

Chorus 3

                D7   **G**   **D7**
Don't you know I heard it through the grapevine,
             G7
Not much longer would you be mine.
        D7   **G** **D7**
Baby, I heard it through the grapevine,
           G7
Ooh, and I'm just about to lose my mind.
           | **Dm** |
Honey, honey, yeah.

| **Dm** | **Dm** | **Dm** ||

Outro

         Dm
||: Honey, honey I know

That you're letting me go. :|| *Repeat to fade with vocal ad lib.*

I Wish

Words & Music by
Stevie Wonder

Chords: Dm7, G7, A7, B7, Em7, Gm6, A7#9aug, Dm

Capo first fret

Intro

‖: Dm7 G7 | Dm7 G7 | Dm7 G7 | Dm7 G7 :‖

Verse 1

    Dm7   G7
Lookin' back on when
    Dm7   G7   Dm7 G7 | Dm7 G7 |
I was a little nappy-headed boy,
    Dm7   G7   Dm7
Then my only worry was,
               G7   Dm7 G7 | Dm7 G7 ‖
For Christmas what would be my toy.

Bridge 1

    A7   B7   Em7   Gm6
Even though we sometimes would not get a thing,
    A7   B7   Em7   A7#9aug
We were happy with the joy that they would bring.

Verse 2

    Dm7   G7
Sneakin' out the back door
    Dm7   G7   Dm7 G7 | Dm7 G7 |
To hang out with those hoodlum friends of mine,
    Dm7   G7
Greeted at the back door with,
     Dm7   G7   Dm7 G7 | Dm7 G7 ‖
"I thought I told you not to go outside".

Bridge 2

    A7   B7   Em7   Gm6
Tryin' your best to bring that water to your eye,
    A7   B7   Em7   A7#9aug
Thinkin' it might stop her from whuppin' your behind.

© Copyright 1976 Jobete Music Company Incorporated & Black Bull Music Incorporated, USA.
Jobete Music (UK) Limited/EMI Music Publishing Limited,
127 Charing Cross Road, London WC2 for the United Kingdom and the Republic of Ireland.
All Rights Reserved. International Copyright Secured.

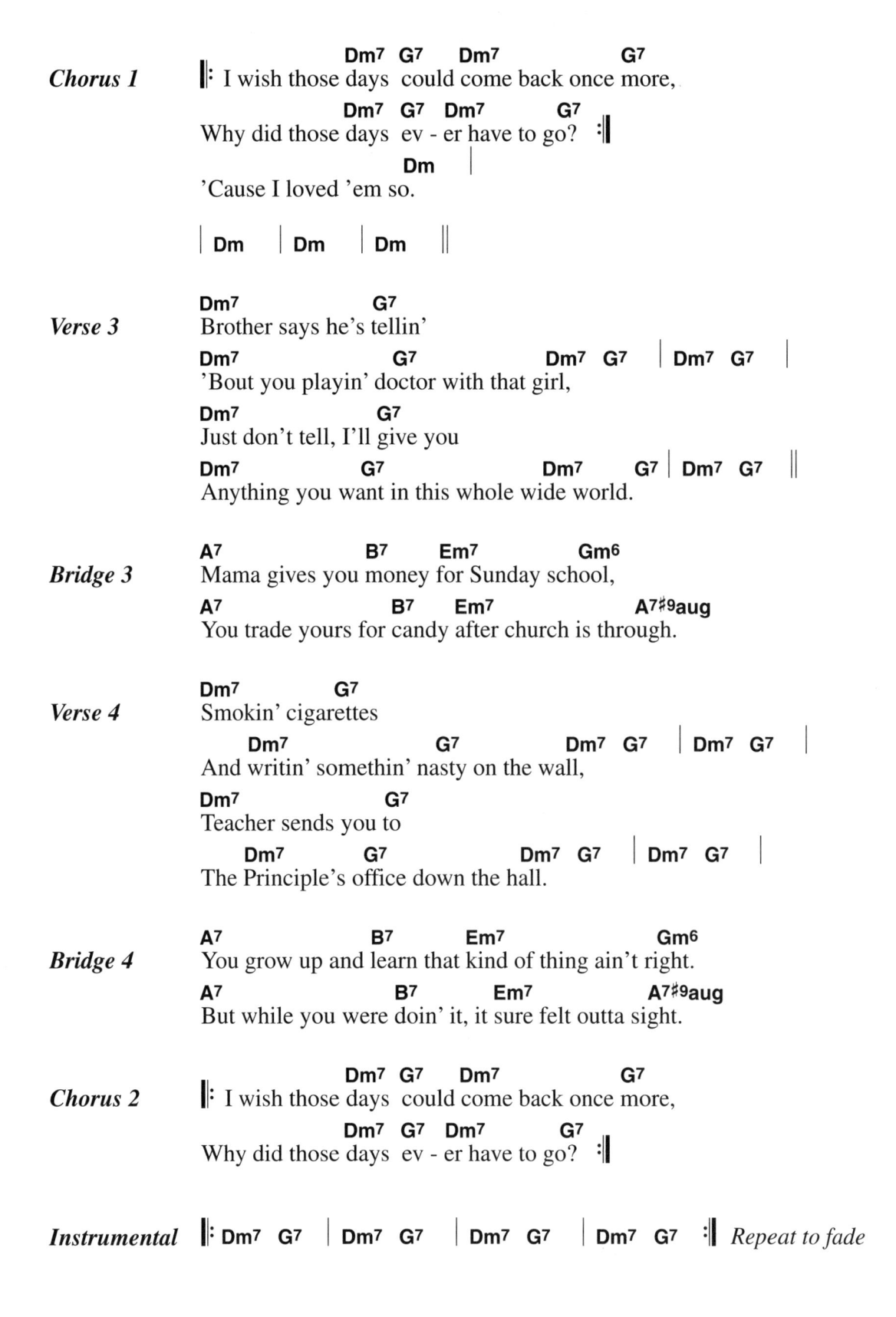

Chorus 1

     Dm7 G7 Dm7   G7
‖: I wish those days could come back once more,
       Dm7 G7 Dm7   G7
Why did those days ev - er have to go? :‖
          Dm
'Cause I loved 'em so.

| Dm | Dm | Dm ‖

Verse 3

Dm7   G7
Brother says he's tellin'
Dm7   G7   Dm7 G7 | Dm7 G7 |
'Bout you playin' doctor with that girl,
Dm7   G7
Just don't tell, I'll give you
Dm7   G7   Dm7 G7 | Dm7 G7 ‖
Anything you want in this whole wide world.

Bridge 3

A7   B7   Em7   Gm6
Mama gives you money for Sunday school,
A7   B7   Em7   A7♯9aug
You trade yours for candy after church is through.

Verse 4

Dm7   G7
Smokin' cigarettes
  Dm7   G7   Dm7 G7 | Dm7 G7 |
And writin' somethin' nasty on the wall,
Dm7   G7
Teacher sends you to
  Dm7   G7   Dm7 G7 | Dm7 G7 |
The Principle's office down the hall.

Bridge 4

A7   B7   Em7   Gm6
You grow up and learn that kind of thing ain't right.
A7   B7   Em7   A7♯9aug
But while you were doin' it, it sure felt outta sight.

Chorus 2

     Dm7 G7 Dm7   G7
‖: I wish those days could come back once more,
       Dm7 G7 Dm7   G7
Why did those days ev - er have to go? :‖

Instrumental

‖: Dm7 G7 | Dm7 G7 | Dm7 G7 | Dm7 G7 :‖ *Repeat to fade*

I'd Rather Go Blind

Words & Music by
Ellington Jordan & Billy Foster

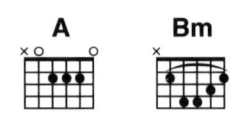

```
  A        Bm
```

Intro | A | Bm | Bm | A ||

Verse 1
       A   Bm
Something told me it was o - ver, (yeah),
                 A
When I saw you and her talking.
                           Bm
Something deep down in my soul said "cry girl,"
                        A
When I saw you and that girl   walking out.

Chorus 1
    A
Ooh, I would rather,
               Bm
I would rather go blind, boy

Than to see you
              A
Walk away from me, child, no.

Ooh, so you see I love you so much,
Bm
   But I don't want

To watch you leave me, babe.

Most of all, I just don't,
      A
I just don't want to be free, no.

© Copyright 1968 Arc Music Corporation, USA.
Jewel Music Publishing Company Limited, 22 Denmark Street, London WC2.
All Rights Reserved. International Copyright Secured

Verse 2

         A   **Bm**
Ooh, ooh, I was just, I was just,

I was just sitting here thinking
                          A
Of your kiss and your warm embrace, yeah.

When the reflection in the glass
      Bm
That I held to my lips now, babe (yeah, yeah),

Revealed the tears
        A
That was on my face, yeah, ooh.

Chorus 2

  A
   And baby, baby I'd rather ,
Bm
I'd rather be blind, boy,

Than to see you walk away,
            A
See you walk away from me, yeah, ooh.
                             Bm
Baby, baby, baby, I'd rather be blind now.
                                Fade out

In The Midnight Hour

Words by Wilson Pickett
Music by Steve Cropper

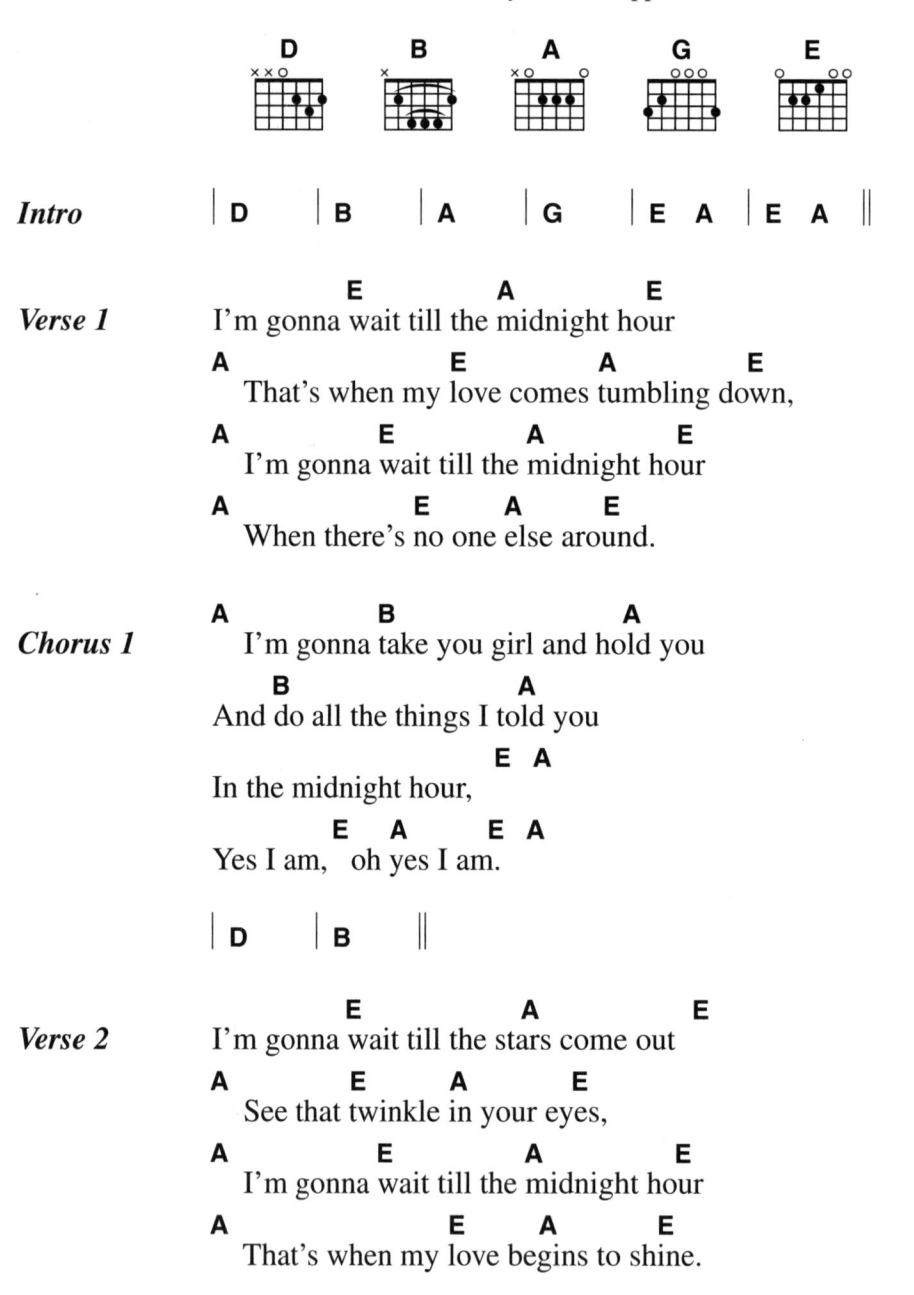

D   B   A   G   E

Intro | D | B | A G | E A | E A ||

Verse 1
        E   A   E
I'm gonna wait till the midnight hour
A   E   A   E
That's when my love comes tumbling down,
A   E   A   E
I'm gonna wait till the midnight hour
A   E   A   E
When there's no one else around.

Chorus 1
A   B   A
I'm gonna take you girl and hold you
B   A
And do all the things I told you
                 E A
In the midnight hour,
      E A   E A
Yes I am, oh yes I am.

| D | B ||

Verse 2
        E   A   E
I'm gonna wait till the stars come out
A   E   A   E
See that twinkle in your eyes,
A   E   A   E
I'm gonna wait till the midnight hour
A   E   A   E
That's when my love begins to shine.

© Copyright 1965 Cotillion Music Incorporated & East Publications Incorporated, USA.
Carlin Music Corporation, Iron Bridge House, 3 Bridge Approach, London NW1 for the British Commonwealth
(excluding Canada and Australasia), the Republic of Ireland and Israel.
All Rights Reserved. International Copyright Secured.

Chorus 2

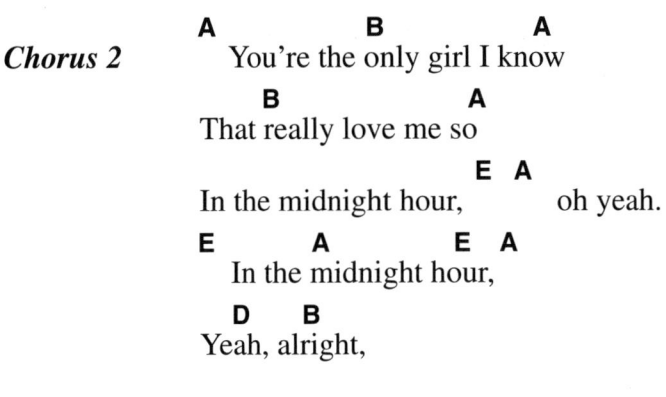

    A   B   A
You're the only girl I know
    B   A
That really love me so
                    E A
In the midnight hour,   oh yeah.
E   A   E A
  In the midnight hour,
  D B
Yeah, alright,

Play it for me one time, now.

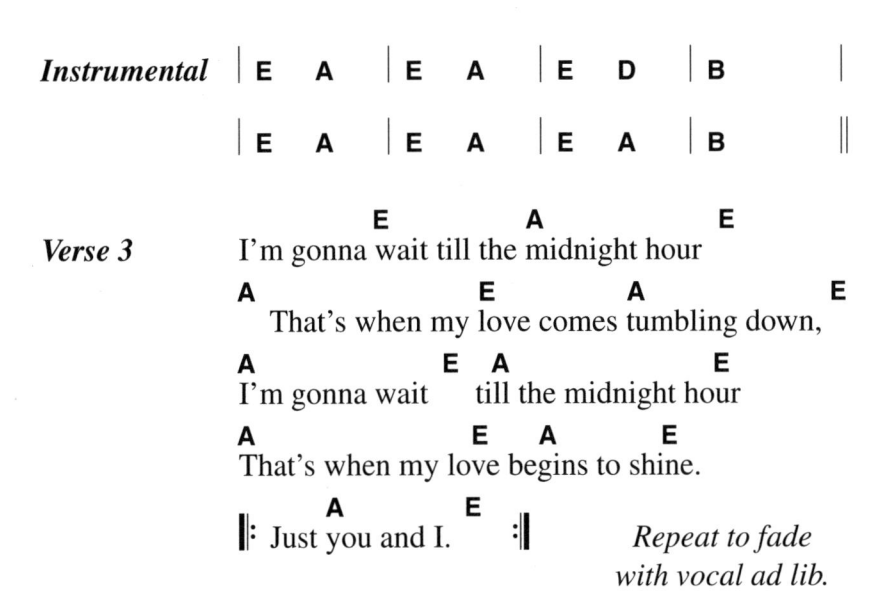

Instrumental | E A | E A | E D | B |

                      | E A | E A | E A | B ||

Verse 3

           E   A   E
I'm gonna wait till the midnight hour
A   E   A   E
  That's when my love comes tumbling down,
A   E A   E
I'm gonna wait   till the midnight hour
A   E   A   E
That's when my love begins to shine.
     A   E
||: Just you and I. :|| *Repeat to fade*
                                    with vocal ad lib.

Midnight Train To Georgia

Words & Music by
Jim Weatherly

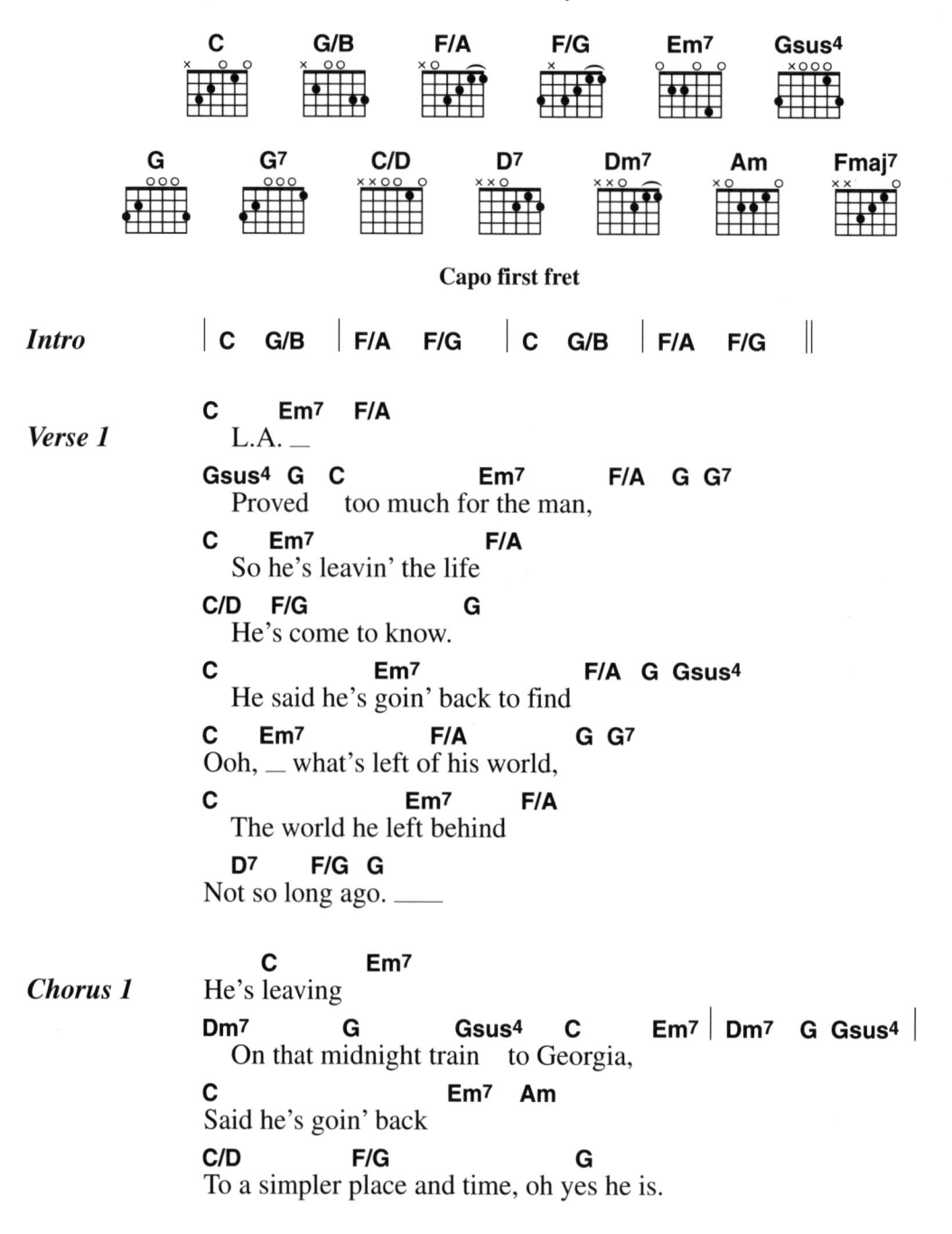

[Chord diagrams: C, G/B, F/A, F/G, Em7, Gsus4, G, G7, C/D, D7, Dm7, Am, Fmaj7]

Capo first fret

Intro | C G/B | F/A F/G | C G/B | F/A F/G ||

Verse 1
     C   Em7   F/A
     L.A. __
Gsus4 G C   Em7   F/A G G7
Proved   too much for the man,
  C   Em7   F/A
So he's leavin' the life
C/D F/G   G
He's come to know.
  C   Em7   F/A G Gsus4
He said he's goin' back to find
  C   Em7   F/A   G G7
Ooh, __ what's left of his world,
  C   Em7   F/A
The world he left behind
  D7   F/G G
Not so long ago. ___

Chorus 1
           C   Em7
     He's leaving
Dm7   G   Gsus4 C   Em7 | Dm7 G Gsus4 |
  On that midnight train   to Georgia,
C   Em7 Am
Said he's goin' back
C/D   F/G   G
To a simpler place and time, oh yes he is.

© Copyright 1976 Keca Music Incorporated, USA.
Universal Music Publishing Limited, 77 Fulham Palace Road, London W6.
All Rights Reserved. International Copyright Secured.

cont.

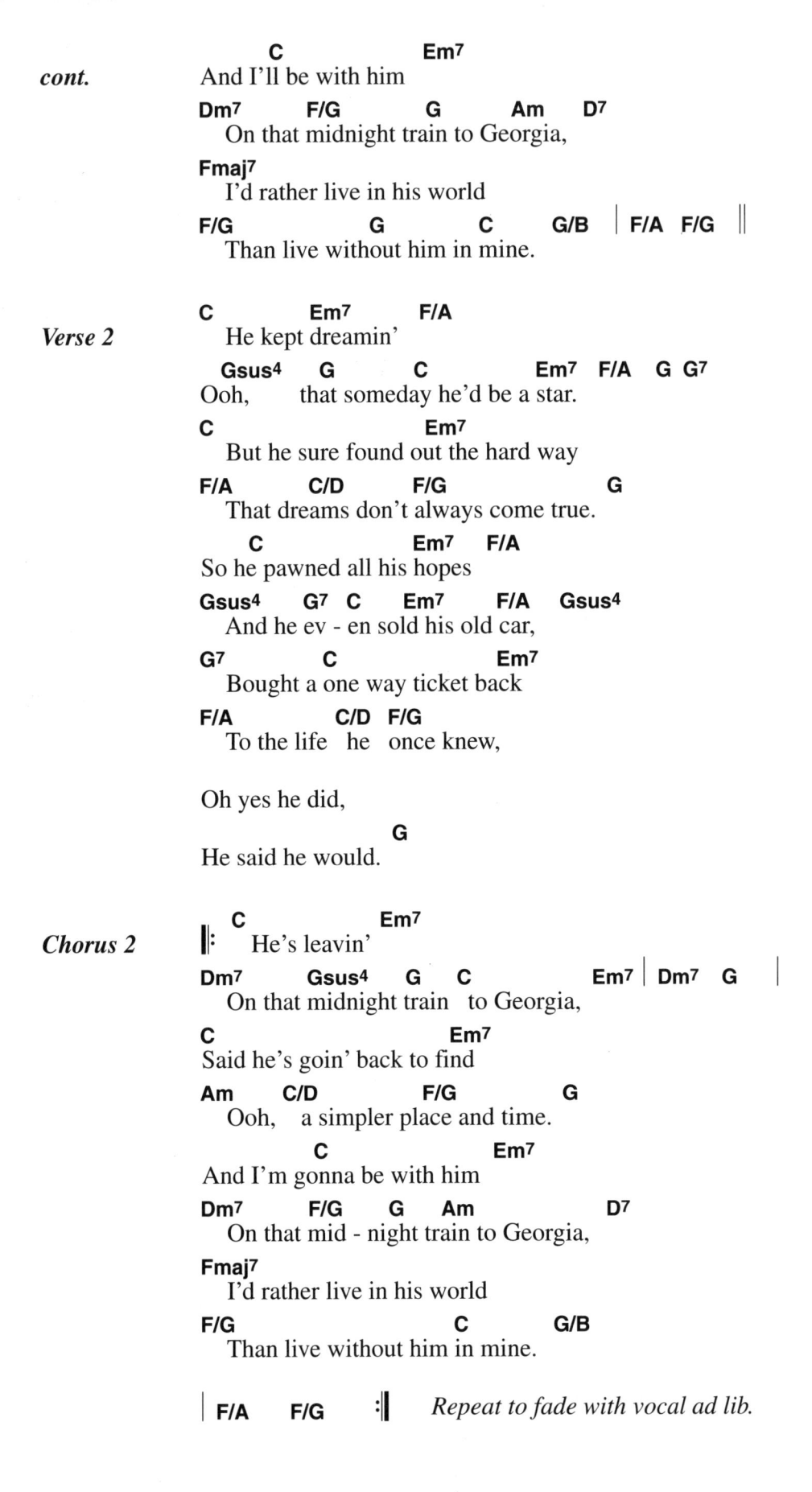

       C   Em7
And I'll be with him

Dm7   F/G   G   Am   D7
  On that midnight train to Georgia,

Fmaj7
  I'd rather live in his world

F/G   G   C   G/B | F/A F/G ||
  Than live without him in mine.

Verse 2

     C   Em7   F/A
  He kept dreamin'

  Gsus4   G   C   Em7 F/A G G7
Ooh,   that someday he'd be a star.

C   Em7
  But he sure found out the hard way

F/A   C/D   F/G   G
  That dreams don't always come true.

    C   Em7   F/A
So he pawned all his hopes

Gsus4 G7 C   Em7   F/A   Gsus4
  And he ev - en sold his old car,

G7   C   Em7
  Bought a one way ticket back

F/A   C/D F/G
  To the life he once knew,

Oh yes he did,

            G
He said he would.

Chorus 2

  ||: C   Em7
    He's leavin'

Dm7   Gsus4 G   C   Em7 | Dm7 G |
  On that midnight train   to Georgia,

C   Em7
Said he's goin' back to find

Am   C/D   F/G   G
  Ooh,   a simpler place and time.

         C   Em7
And I'm gonna be with him

Dm7   F/G   G   Am   D7
  On that mid - night train to Georgia,

Fmaj7
  I'd rather live in his world

F/G   C   G/B
  Than live without him in mine.

    | F/A   F/G   :|| *Repeat to fade with vocal ad lib.*

I Say A Little Prayer

Words by Hal David
Music by Burt Bacharach

Intro | F#m | Bm7 | Bm7 | E | Amaj7 | D | C#7 |

Verse 1
F#m   Bm7
The moment I wake up,
          E   Amaj7
Before I put on my make-up
   D   C#7
I say a little prayer for you.
F#m   Bm7
And while combing my hair now
                  E   Amaj7
And wond'ring what dress to wear now,
   D   C#7
I say a little prayer for you.

Chorus 1
     D   E   C#m   F#m
Forever, forever, you'll stay in my heart
     Bm/A   A7   D   E
And I will love   you forever and ever.
      C#m   F#m
We never will part,
          Bm/A   A7
Oh, how I'll love   you.
     D   E   C#m   F#m
Together, together, that's how it must be.
            Bm/A   A7
To live without   you
       D   D/E   C#7
Would only mean heart-break for me.

© Copyright 1966 Blue Seas Music Incorporated/Casa David Music Incorporated, USA.
Universal/MCA Music Limited, 77 Fulham Palace Road, London W6 (50%)/
Windswept Pacific Music Limited, Hope House, 40 St. Peter's Road, London W6 (50%).
All Rights Reserved. International Copyright Secured.

Verse 2

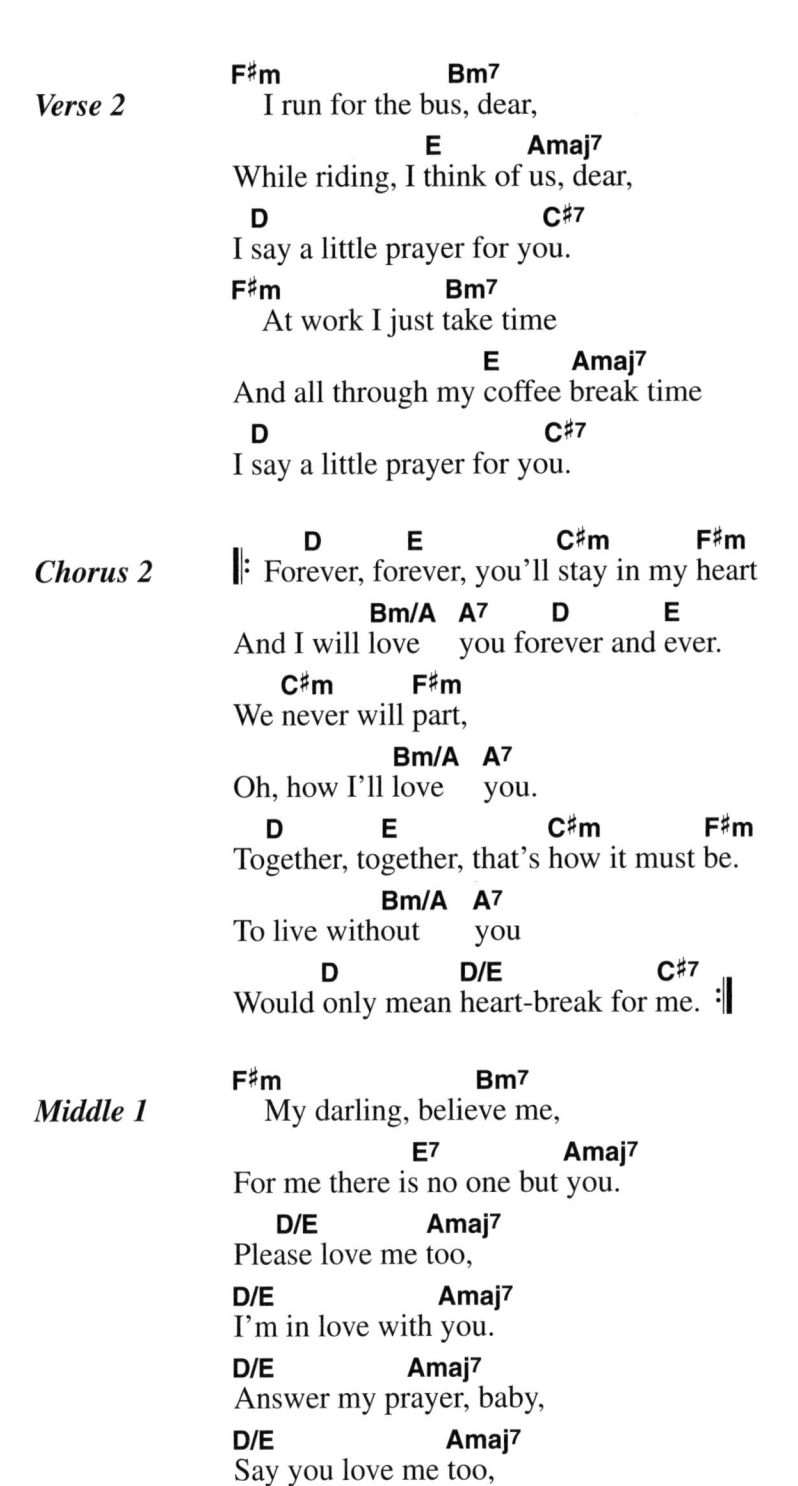

      F♯m   Bm7
   I run for the bus, dear,
                 E   Amaj7
While riding, I think of us, dear,
 D   C♯7
I say a little prayer for you.
F♯m   Bm7
  At work I just take time
                    E   Amaj7
And all through my coffee break time
 D   C♯7
I say a little prayer for you.

Chorus 2

        D   E   C♯m   F♯m
‖: Forever, forever, you'll stay in my heart
           Bm/A A7   D   E
And I will love   you forever and ever.
   C♯m   F♯m
We never will part,
          Bm/A A7
Oh, how I'll love   you.
     D   E   C♯m   F♯m
Together, together, that's how it must be.
          Bm/A A7
To live without   you
       D   D/E   C♯7
Would only mean heart-break for me. :‖

Middle 1

F♯m   Bm7
  My darling, believe me,
        E7   Amaj7
For me there is no one but you.
 D/E   Amaj7
Please love me too,
D/E   Amaj7
I'm in love with you.
D/E   Amaj7
Answer my prayer, baby,
D/E   Amaj7
Say you love me too,
 D/E   Amaj7
Answer my prayer, please.

Chorus 3

     D   E   C♯m   F♯m
Forever, forever, you'll stay in my heart
               Bm/A A7   D   E
And I will love   you forever and ever.
    C♯m   F♯m
We never will part,
            Bm/A A7
Oh, how I'll love   you.
     D   E   C♯m   F♯m
Together, together, that's how it must be.
         Bm/A A7
To live without   you
       D   D/E   C♯7
Would only mean heart-break for me.

Middle 2

 F♯m   Bm7
  My darling, believe me,
           E7   Amaj7
For me there is no one but you.
  D/E   Amaj7
Please love me too.
  D/E   Amaj7
𝄆 This is my prayer,
  D/E   Amaj7
Answer my prayer now, baby. 𝄇   *Repeat to fade*
                                          with vocal ad lib.

Rescue Me

Words & Music by
Carl Smith & Raynard Miner

```
    A      D/A      D      D/E     G      Em
```

Intro | A   A   A | D/A   A | D/A   D | D/E ||

Verse 1
      A
Rescue me
           D
Or take me in your arms,
     G
Rescue me
           Em
I want your tender charms,
      A   D
'Cause I'm lonely and I'm blue,
    G
I need you
       Em
And your love too,

Come on and rescue me.

Chorus 1
A   D
Come on baby and rescue me,
A   D
Come on baby and rescue me,
A   D
'Cause I need you by my side,
          D/E
Can't you see that I'm lonely.

© Copyright 1965 Chevis Music Incorporated, USA.
Jewel Music Publishing Company Limited, 22 Denmark Street, London WC2.
All Rights Reserved. International Copyright Secured.

Verse 2

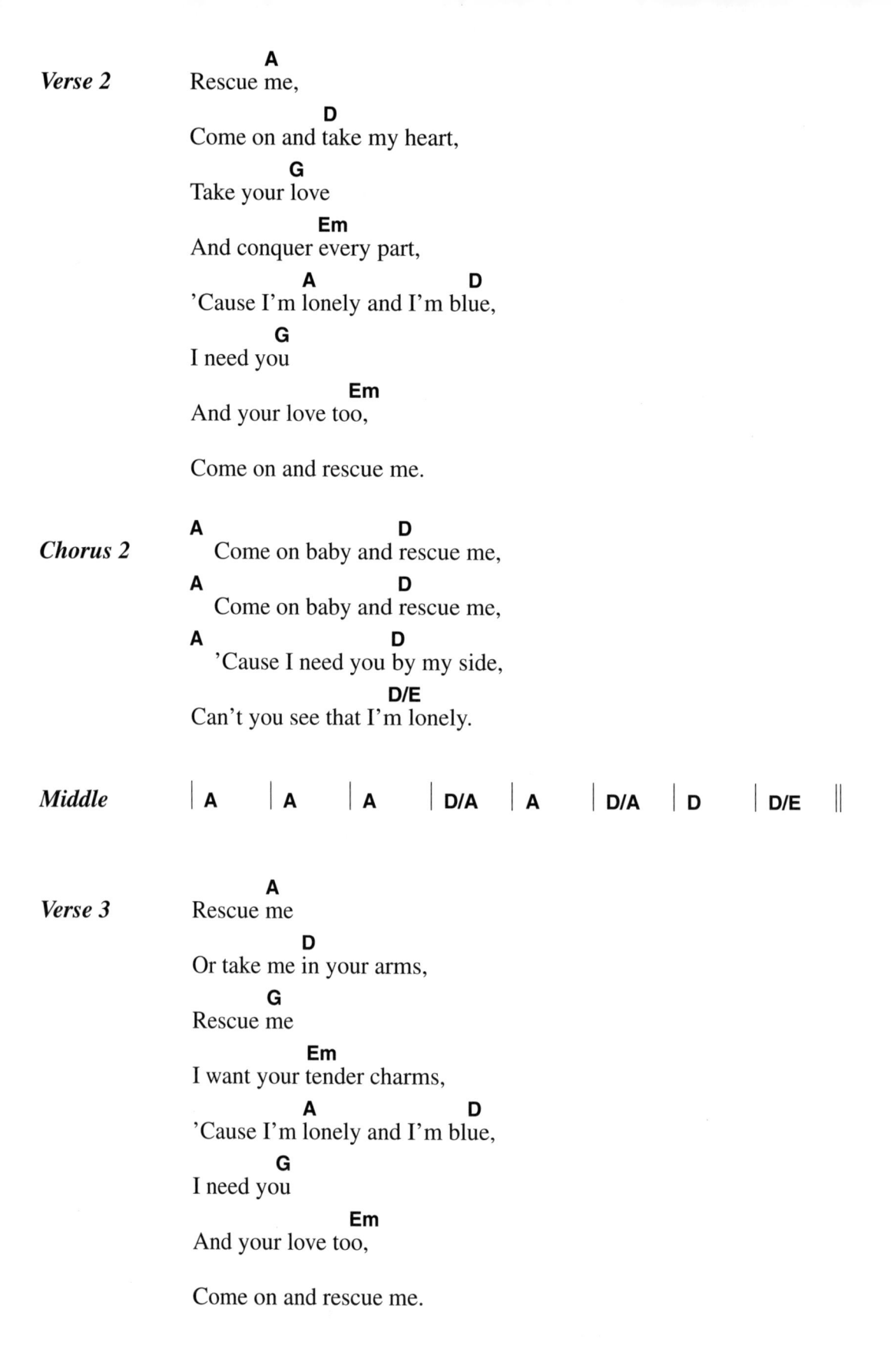

    A
Rescue me,

             D
Come on and take my heart,

        G
Take your love

              Em
And conquer every part,

        A   **D**
'Cause I'm lonely and I'm blue,

    G
I need you

            Em
And your love too,

Come on and rescue me.

Chorus 2

  A   **D**
  Come on baby and rescue me,

A   **D**
  Come on baby and rescue me,

A   **D**
  'Cause I need you by my side,

           D/E
Can't you see that I'm lonely.

Middle

| A | A | A | D/A | A | D/A | D | D/E ||

Verse 3

    A
Rescue me

      D
Or take me in your arms,

    G
Rescue me

        Em
I want your tender charms,

    A   **D**
'Cause I'm lonely and I'm blue,

  G
I need you

        Em
And your love too,

Come on and rescue me.

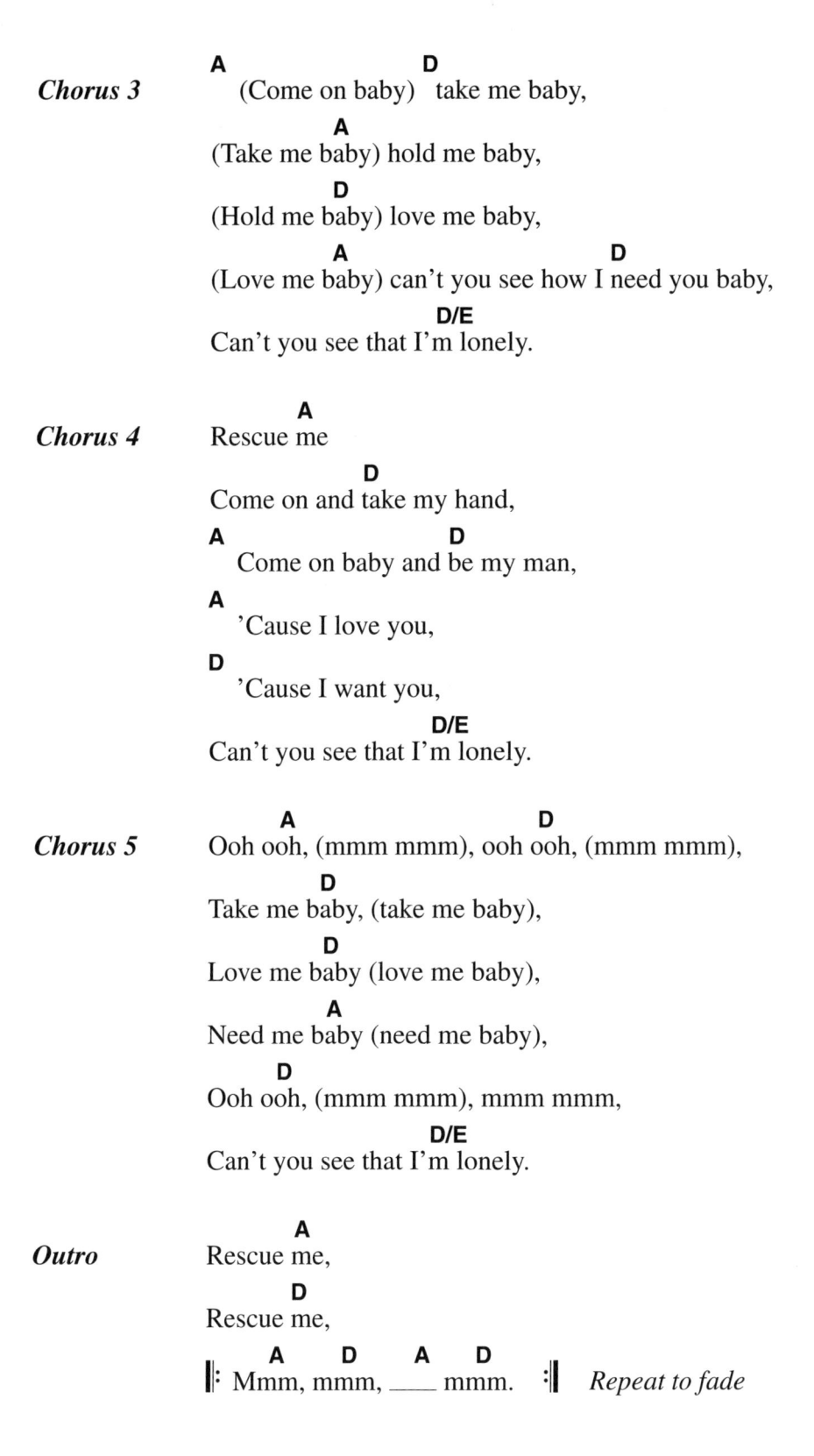

Chorus 3

      A   D
(Come on baby)   take me baby,
               A
(Take me baby) hold me baby,
             D
(Hold me baby) love me baby,
            A   D
(Love me baby) can't you see how I need you baby,
                      D/E
Can't you see that I'm lonely.

Chorus 4

   A
Rescue me
           D
Come on and take my hand,
A   D
Come on baby and be my man,
A
'Cause I love you,
D
'Cause I want you,
                  D/E
Can't you see that I'm lonely.

Chorus 5

   A   D
Ooh ooh, (mmm mmm), ooh ooh, (mmm mmm),
      D
Take me baby, (take me baby),
     D
Love me baby (love me baby),
    A
Need me baby (need me baby),
   D
Ooh ooh, (mmm mmm), mmm mmm,
               D/E
Can't you see that I'm lonely.

Outro

   A
Rescue me,
   D
Rescue me,
𝄆 A   D   A   D 𝄇
Mmm, mmm, ___ mmm.   *Repeat to fade*

Stay With Me Baby

Words & Music by
Jerry Ragovoy & George David Weiss

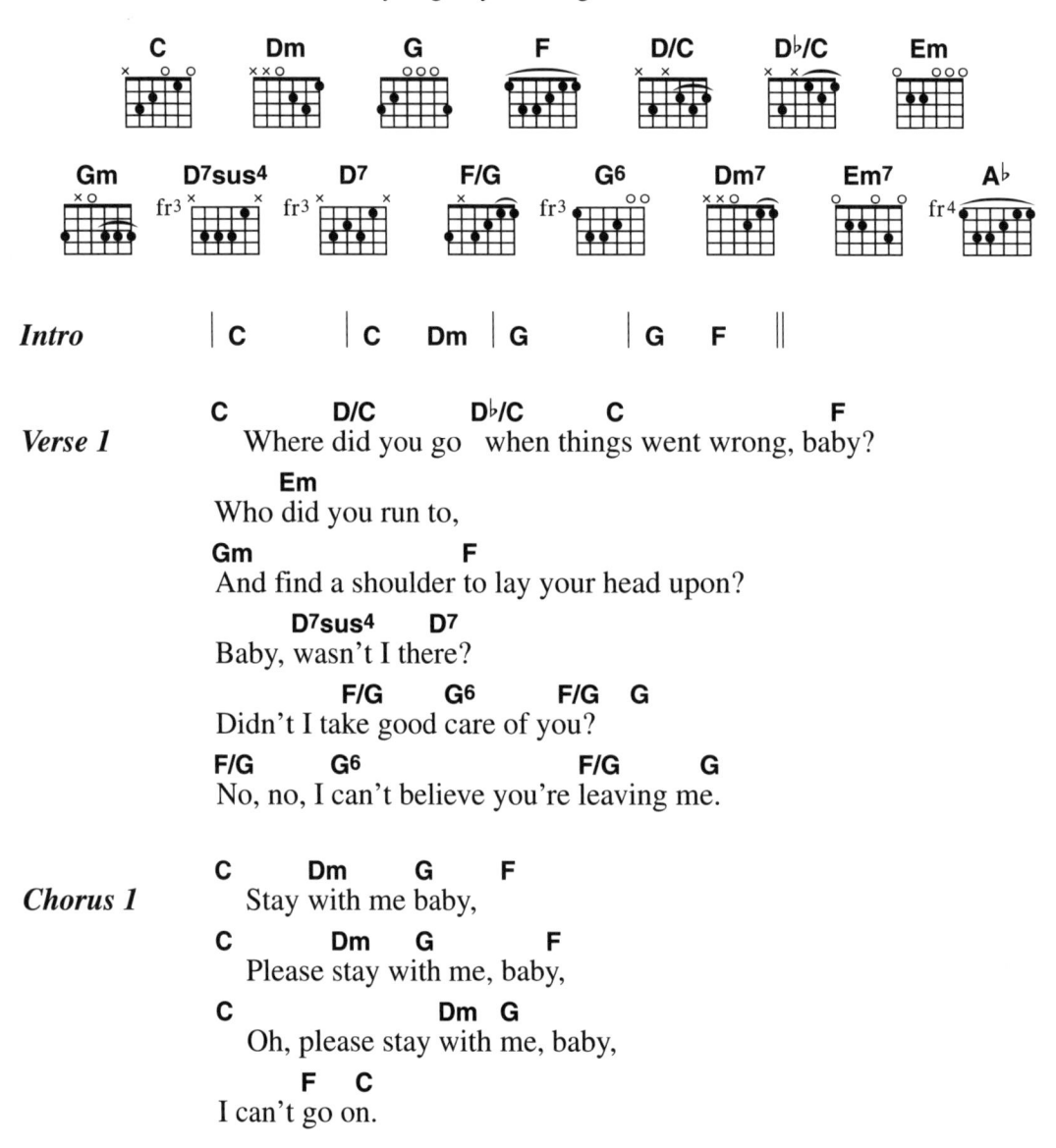

Intro
| C | C Dm | G | G F ||

Verse 1
      C   D/C   D♭/C   C   F
Where did you go   when things went wrong, baby?
      Em
Who did you run to,
  Gm   F
And find a shoulder to lay your head upon?
      D7sus4   D7
Baby, wasn't I there?
         F/G   G6   F/G   G
Didn't I take good care of you?
F/G   G6   F/G   G
No, no, I can't believe you're leaving me.

Chorus 1
     C   Dm   G   F
Stay with me baby,
     C   Dm G   F
Please stay with me, baby,
     C   Dm G
Oh, please stay with me, baby,
    F C
I can't go on.

© Copyright 1966 Abilene Music Incorporated/Memory Lane Music Limited,
22 Denmark Street, London WC2 (50%)/Copyright Control (50%).
All Rights Reserved. International Copyright Secured.

Verse 2

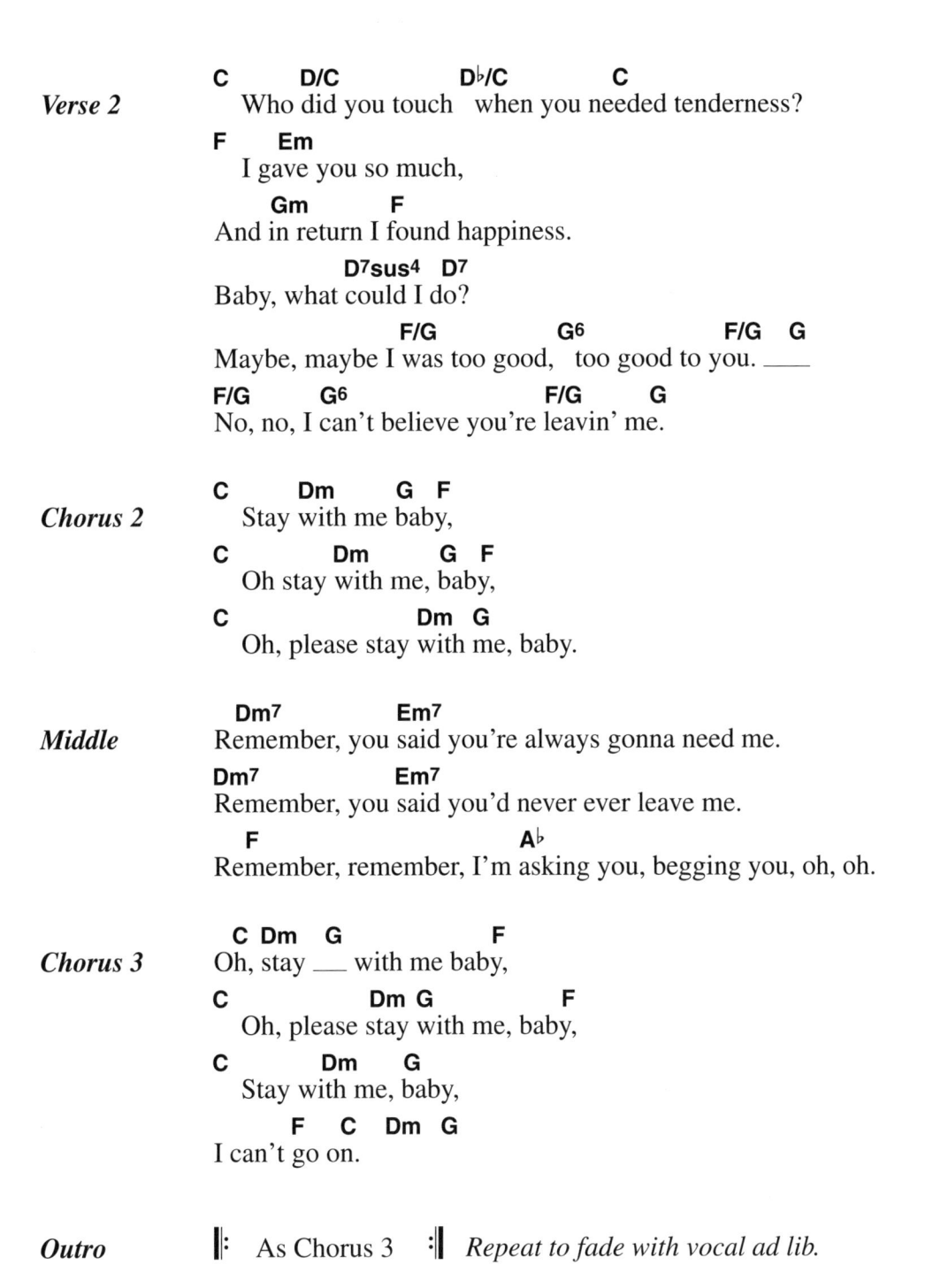

   C D/C   D♭/C C
   Who did you touch when you needed tenderness?
  F Em
  I gave you so much,
   Gm F
  And in return I found happiness.
       D7sus4 D7
  Baby, what could I do?
      F/G   G6   F/G G
  Maybe, maybe I was too good, too good to you. ___
  F/G G6   F/G G
  No, no, I can't believe you're leavin' me.

Chorus 2

   C Dm G F
   Stay with me baby,
   C   Dm   G F
   Oh stay with me, baby,
   C   Dm G
   Oh, please stay with me, baby.

Middle

   Dm7   Em7
   Remember, you said you're always gonna need me.
   Dm7   Em7
   Remember, you said you'd never ever leave me.
     F   A♭
   Remember, remember, I'm asking you, begging you, oh, oh.

Chorus 3

   C Dm G   F
   Oh, stay ___ with me baby,
   C   Dm G   F
   Oh, please stay with me, baby,
   C   Dm G
   Stay with me, baby,
     F C Dm G
   I can't go on.

Outro

   ‖: As Chorus 3 :‖ *Repeat to fade with vocal ad lib.*

Summer Breeze

Words & Music by
James Seals & Darrell Crofts

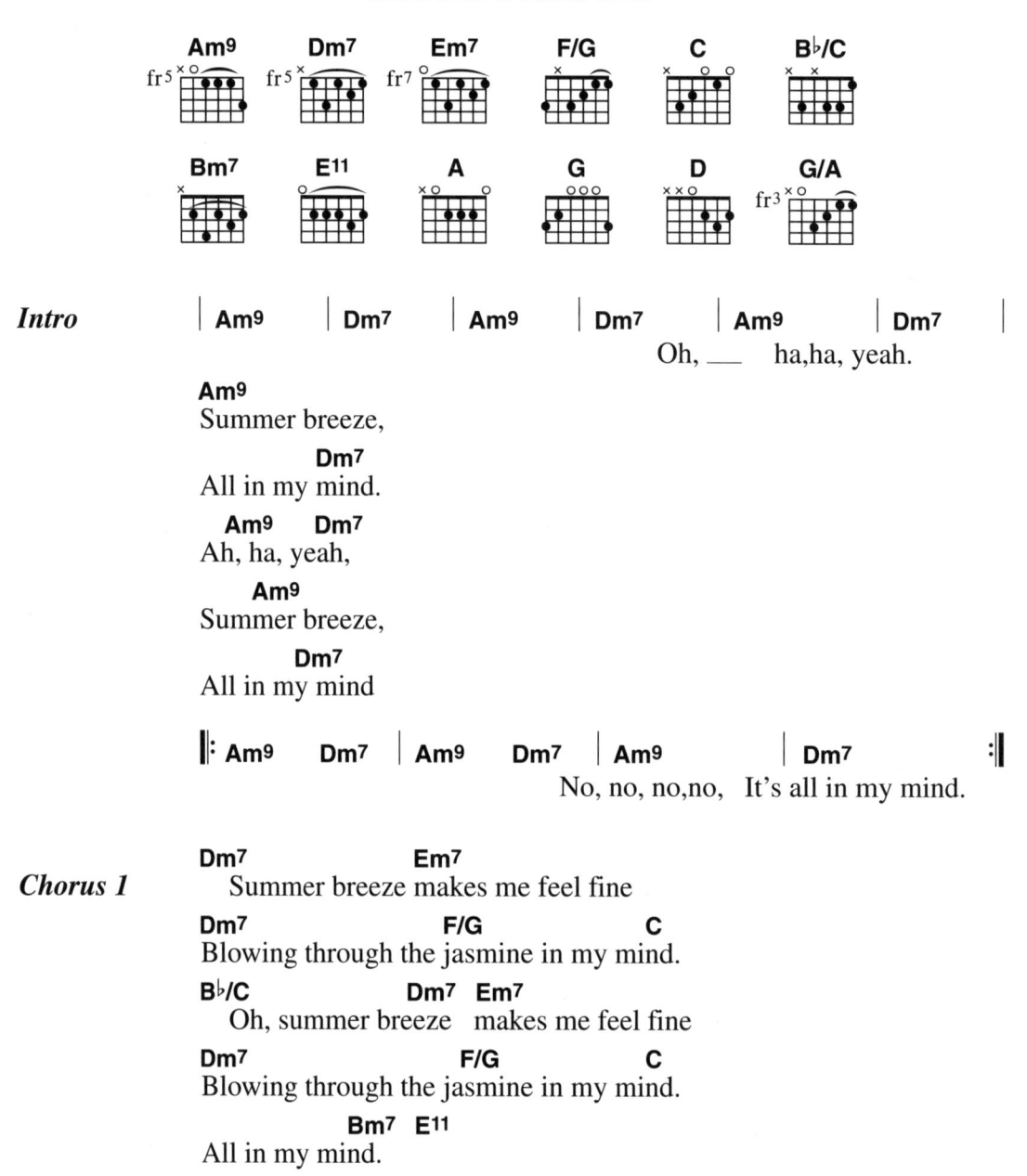

[Chord diagrams: Am9, Dm7, Em7, F/G, C, B♭/C, Bm7, E11, A, G, D, G/A]

Intro | Am9 | Dm7 | Am9 | Dm7 | Am9 | Dm7 |
            Oh, __ ha, ha, yeah.

Am9
Summer breeze,
   Dm7
All in my mind.
   Am9   Dm7
Ah, ha, yeah,
   Am9
Summer breeze,
   Dm7
All in my mind

‖: Am9   Dm7 | Am9   Dm7 | Am9   Dm7 :‖
              No, no, no,no, It's all in my mind.

Chorus 1
Dm7   Em7
Summer breeze makes me feel fine
Dm7   F/G   C
Blowing through the jasmine in my mind.
B♭/C   Dm7   Em7
Oh, summer breeze   makes me feel fine
Dm7   F/G   C
Blowing through the jasmine in my mind.
         Bm7   E11
All in my mind.

© Copyright 1971 Dawnbreaker Music Company & Trousdale Music Publishers Incorporated, USA.
The International Music Network Limited, Independent House, 54 Larkshall Road, London E4 (87.5%)
& Universal/MCA Music Limited, 77 Fulham Palace Road, London W6 (12.5%).
All Rights Reserved. International Copyright Secured.

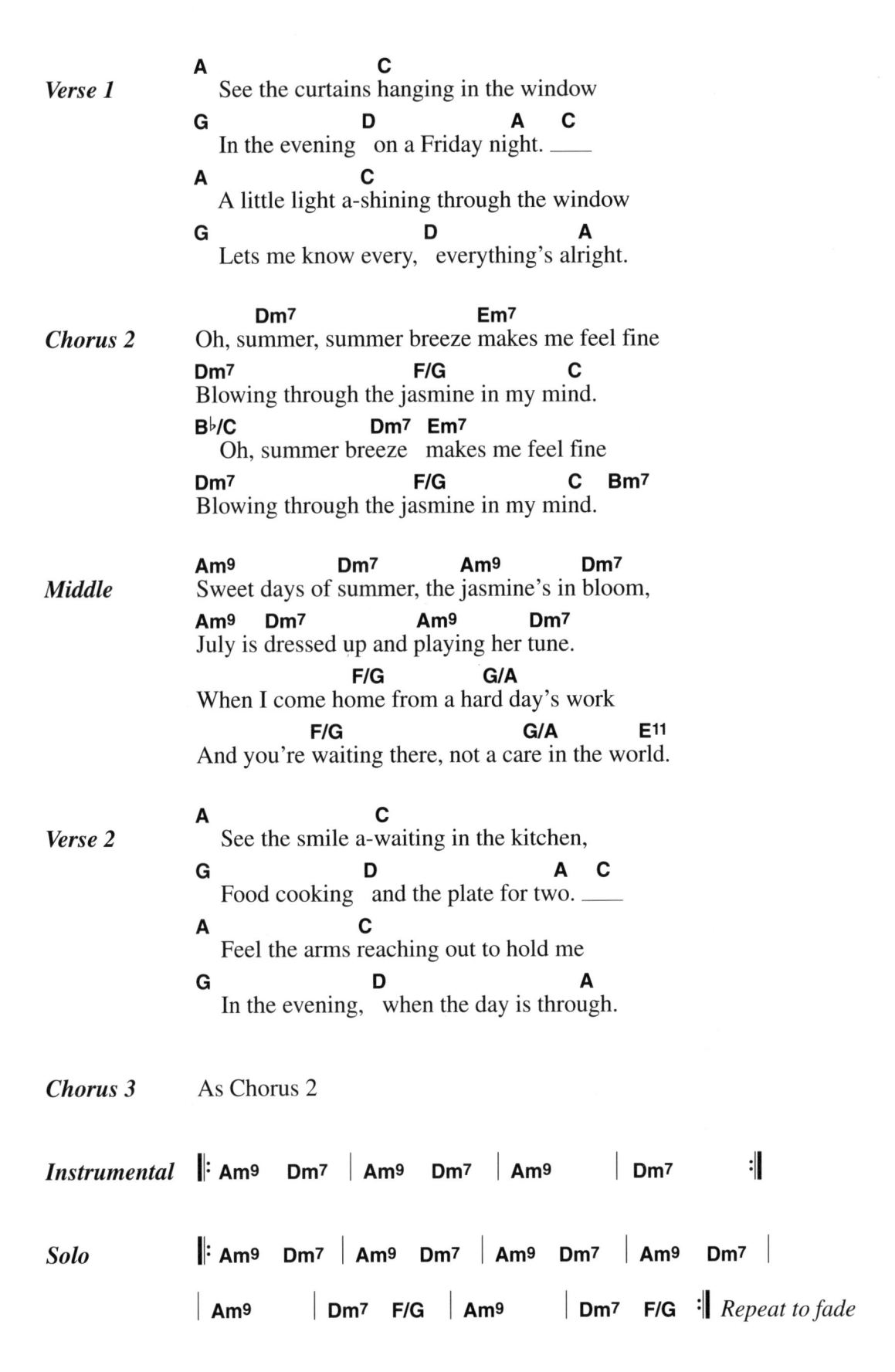

Verse 1

     A   C
See the curtains hanging in the window
G   D   A   C
In the evening   on a Friday night. ____
A   C
A little light a-shining through the window
G   D   A
Lets me know every,   everything's alright.

Chorus 2

         Dm7   Em7
Oh, summer, summer breeze makes me feel fine
Dm7   F/G   C
Blowing through the jasmine in my mind.
B♭/C   Dm7 Em7
Oh, summer breeze   makes me feel fine
Dm7   F/G   C   Bm7
Blowing through the jasmine in my mind.

Middle

Am9   Dm7   Am9   Dm7
Sweet days of summer, the jasmine's in bloom,
Am9 Dm7   Am9   Dm7
July is dressed up and playing her tune.
                  F/G   G/A
When I come home from a hard day's work
            F/G   G/A   E11
And you're waiting there, not a care in the world.

Verse 2

     A   C
See the smile a-waiting in the kitchen,
G   D   A   C
Food cooking   and the plate for two. ____
A   C
Feel the arms reaching out to hold me
G   D   A
In the evening,   when the day is through.

Chorus 3   As Chorus 2

Instrumental   ‖: Am9 Dm7 | Am9 Dm7 | Am9 | Dm7   :‖

Solo   ‖: Am9 Dm7 | Am9 Dm7 | Am9 Dm7 | Am9 Dm7 |

| Am9 | Dm7 F/G | Am9 | Dm7 F/G :‖ *Repeat to fade*

(Take A Little) Piece Of My Heart

Words & Music by
Jerry Ragovoy & Bert Berns

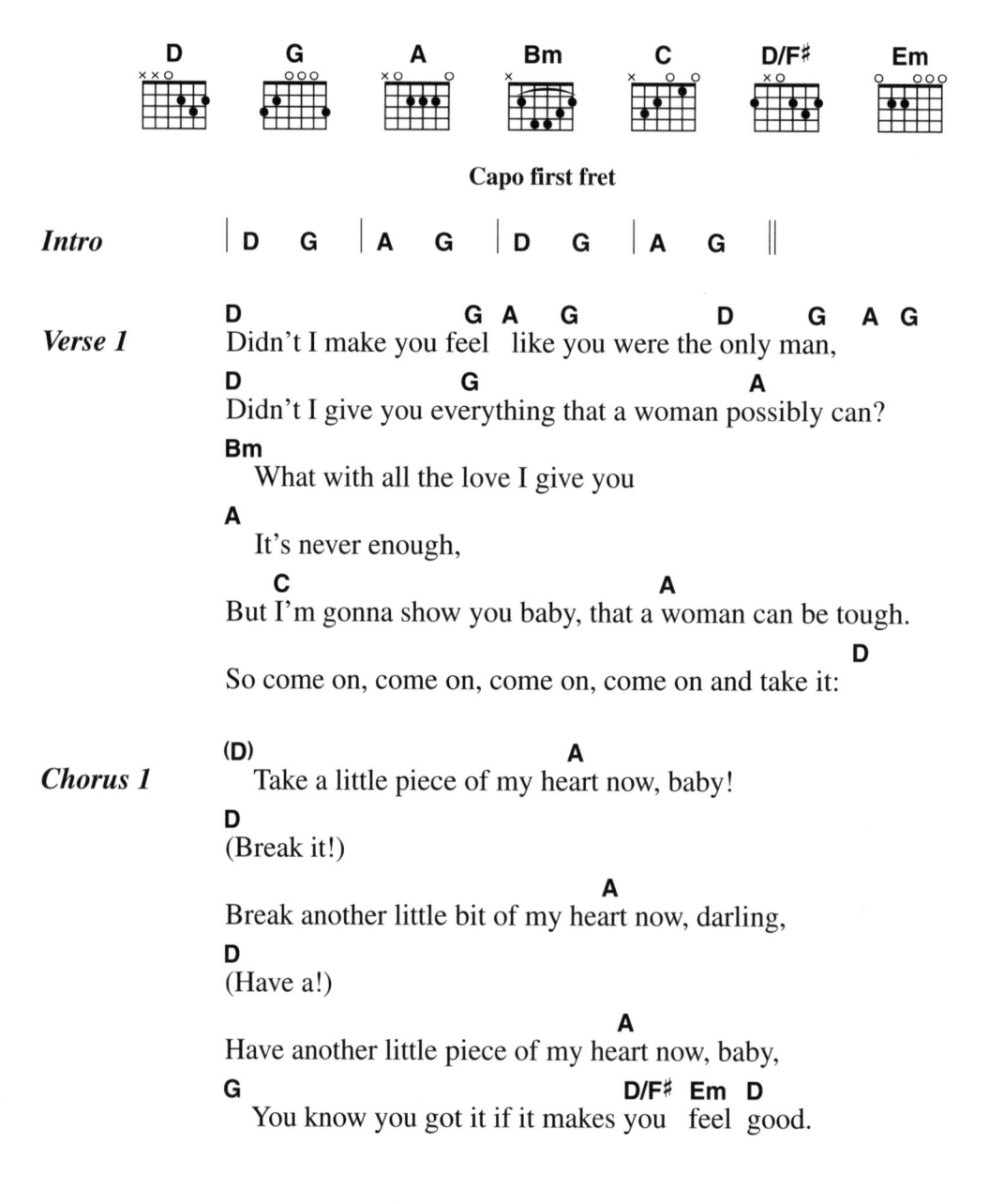

D   G   A   Bm   C   D/F#   Em

Capo first fret

Intro | D G | A G | D G | A G ||

Verse 1

D   G A G   D   G A G
Didn't I make you feel like you were the only man,
D   G   A
Didn't I give you everything that a woman possibly can?
Bm
   What with all the love I give you
A
   It's never enough,
      C   A
But I'm gonna show you baby, that a woman can be tough.
                                    D
So come on, come on, come on, come on and take it:

Chorus 1

(D)   A
Take a little piece of my heart now, baby!
D
(Break it!)
                        A
Break another little bit of my heart now, darling,
D
(Have a!)
                        A
Have another little piece of my heart now, baby,
G   D/F#   Em D
You know you got it if it makes you feel good.

© Copyright 1968 Web IV Music Incorporated, USA.
Sony/ATV Music Publishing (UK) Limited, 10 Great Marlborough Street, London W1.
All Rights Reserved. International Copyright Secured.

Verse 2

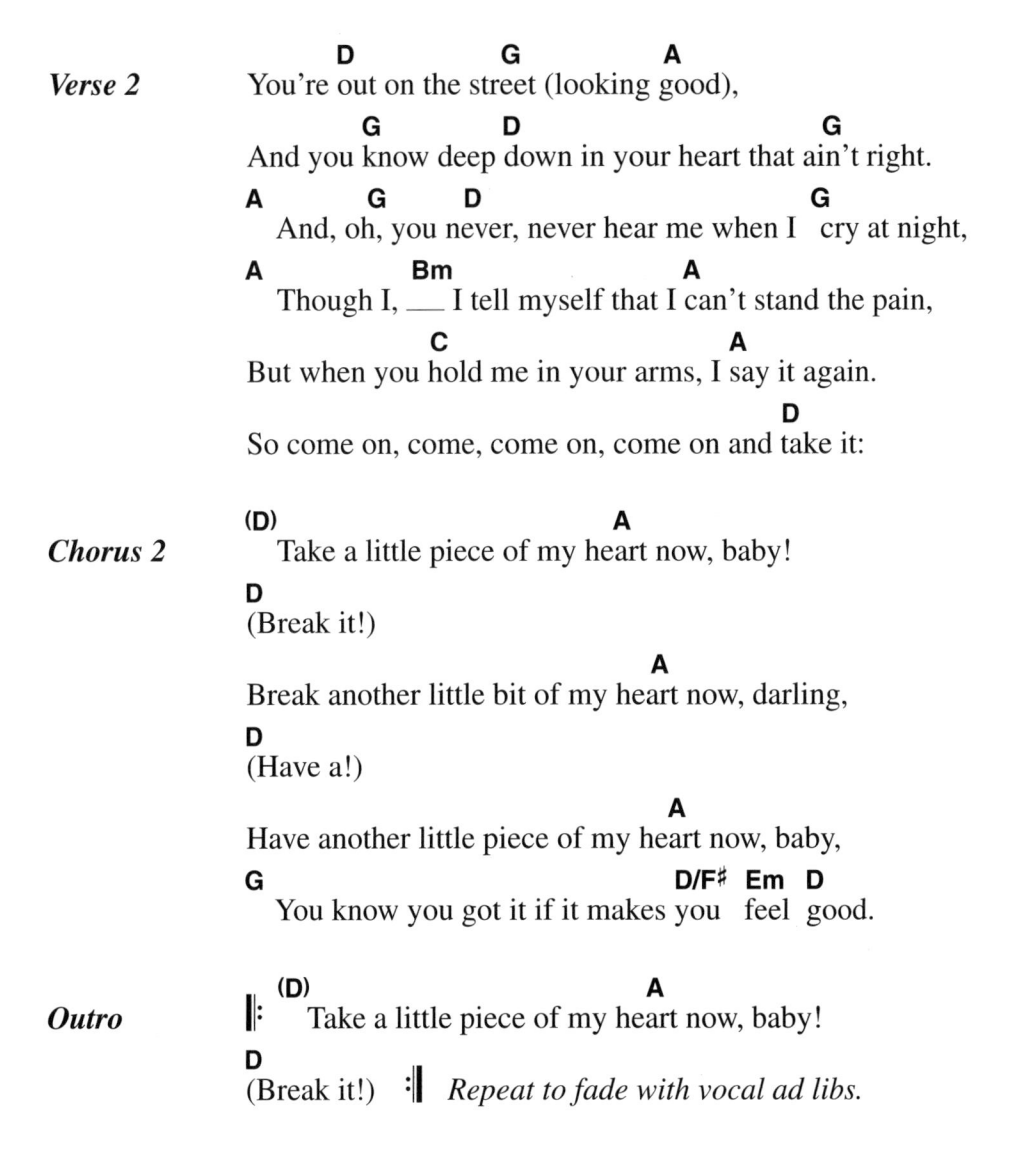

    D   **G**   **A**
  You're out on the street (looking good),
     G   **D**   **G**
  And you know deep down in your heart that ain't right.
  A   **G** **D**   **G**
   And, oh, you never, never hear me when I cry at night,
  A   **Bm**   **A**
   Though I, ___ I tell myself that I can't stand the pain,
       C   **A**
  But when you hold me in your arms, I say it again.
                D
  So come on, come, come on, come on and take it:

Chorus 2

  (D)   **A**
   Take a little piece of my heart now, baby!
  D
  (Break it!)
              A
  Break another little bit of my heart now, darling,
  D
  (Have a!)
             A
  Have another little piece of my heart now, baby,
  G   **D/F♯** **Em** **D**
   You know you got it if it makes you feel good.

Outro

   (D)   **A**
  ‖: Take a little piece of my heart now, baby!
  D
  (Break it!) :‖ *Repeat to fade with vocal ad libs.*

Take Me To The River

Words & Music by
Al Green & Mabon Hodges

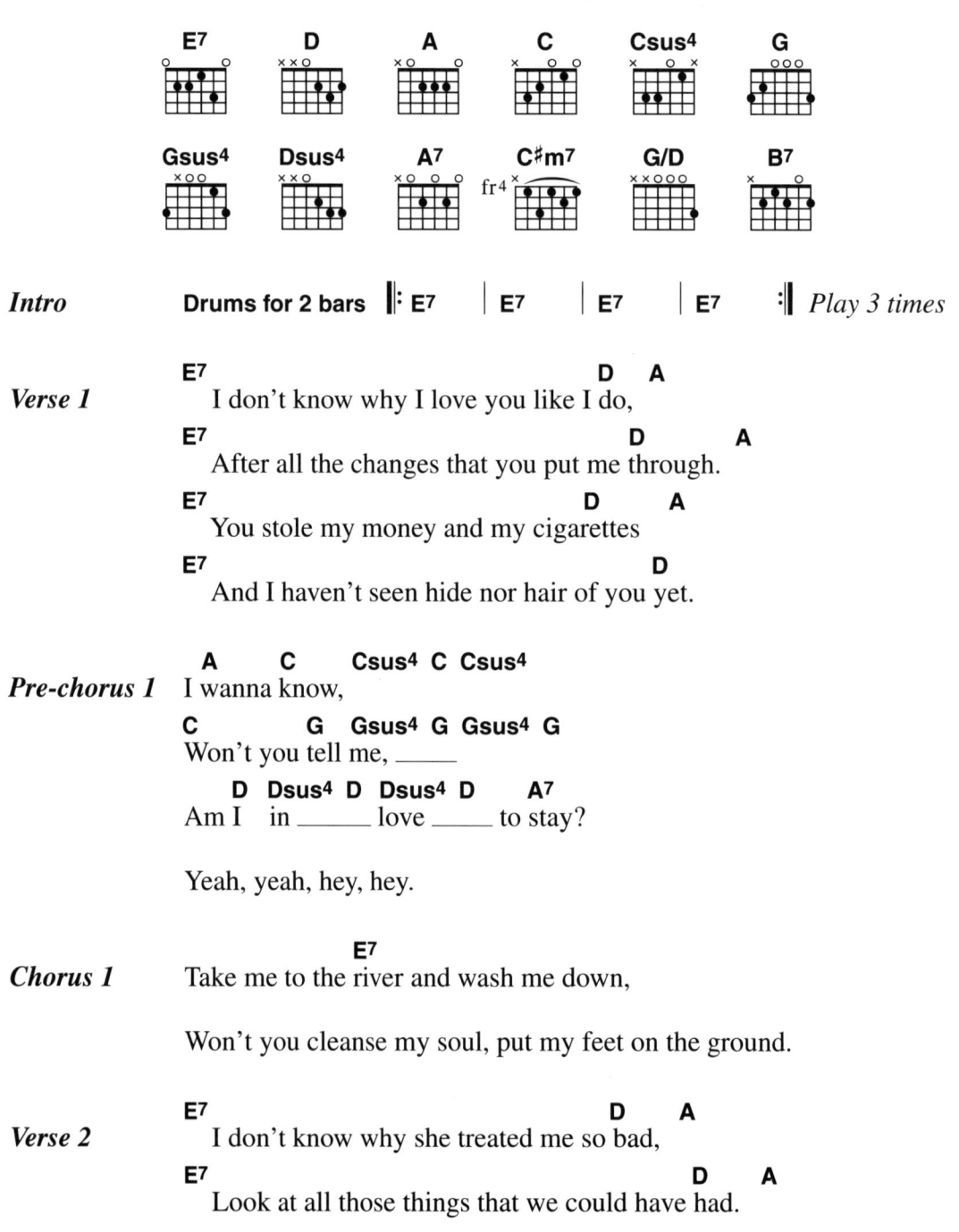

[Chord diagrams: E7, D, A, C, Csus4, G, Gsus4, Dsus4, A7, C#m7, G/D, B7]

Intro   Drums for 2 bars ‖: E7 | E7 | E7 | E7 :‖ *Play 3 times*

Verse 1
E7   D   A
I don't know why I love you like I do,
E7   D   A
After all the changes that you put me through.
E7   D   A
You stole my money and my cigarettes
E7   D
And I haven't seen hide nor hair of you yet.

Pre-chorus 1
  A   C   Csus4 C Csus4
I wanna know,
C   G   Gsus4 G Gsus4 G
Won't you tell me, ____
      D Dsus4 D Dsus4 D   A7
Am I in ____ love ____ to stay?

Yeah, yeah, hey, hey.

Chorus 1
                            E7
Take me to the river and wash me down,

Won't you cleanse my soul, put my feet on the ground.

Verse 2
E7   D   A
I don't know why she treated me so bad,
E7   D   A
Look at all those things that we could have had.

© Copyright 1973 Jec Music Publishing Company & Al Green Music Incorporated, USA.
Rondor Music (London) Limited, 10a Parsons Green, London SW6 (75%)/
Burlington Music Company Limited, Griffin House, 161 Hammersmith Road, London W6 (25%).
All Rights Reserved. International Copyright Secured.

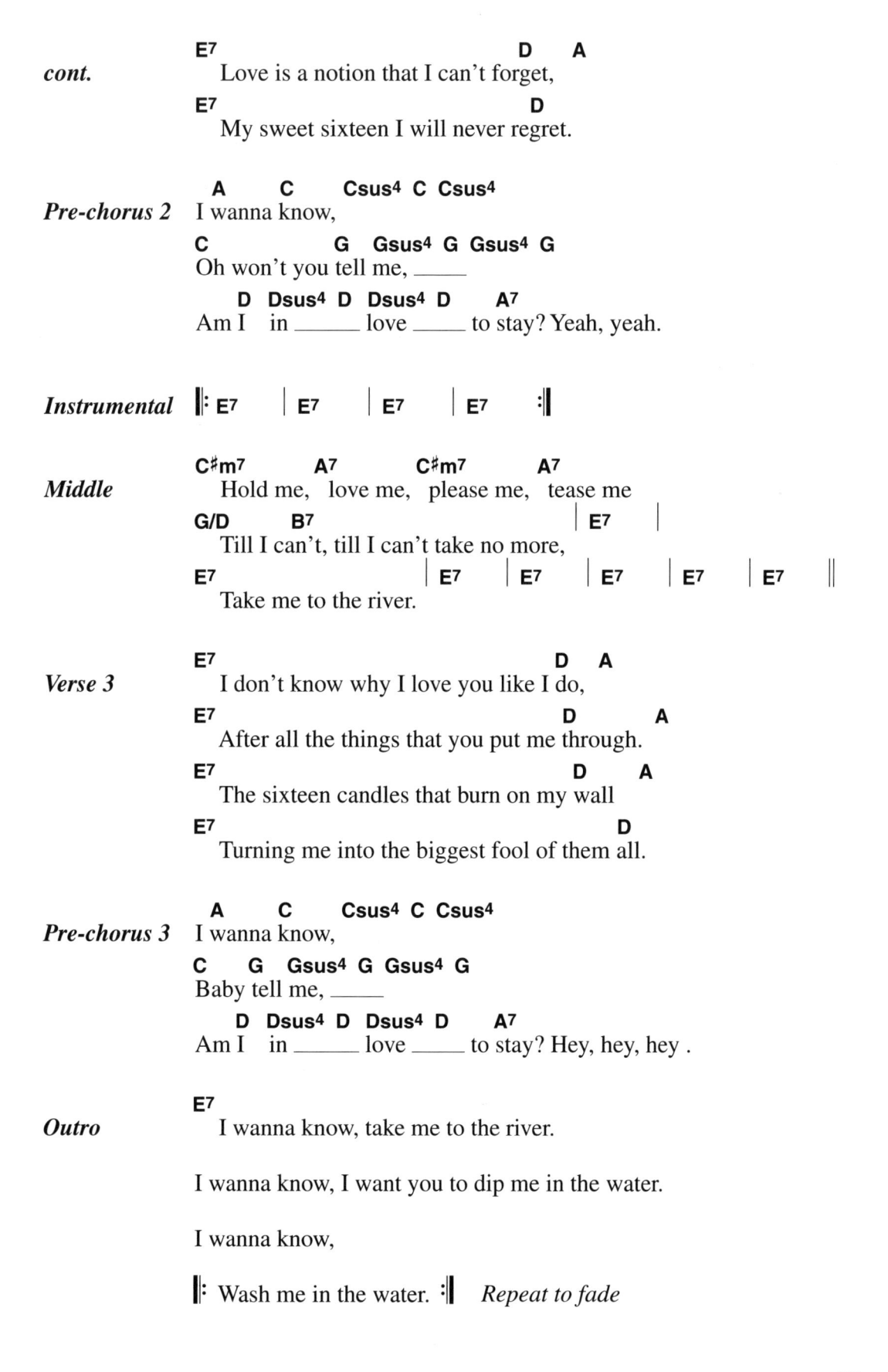

	E7 D A
cont.	Love is a notion that I can't forget,
	E7 D
	My sweet sixteen I will never regret.

	A C Csus4 C Csus4
Pre-chorus 2	I wanna know,
	C G Gsus4 G Gsus4 G
	Oh won't you tell me, _____
	D Dsus4 D Dsus4 D A7
	Am I in ____ love ____ to stay? Yeah, yeah.

Instrumental	‖: E7	E7	E7	E7 :‖

	C#m7 A7 C#m7 A7
Middle	Hold me, love me, please me, tease me
	G/D B7	E7	
	Till I can't, till I can't take no more,
	E7	E7	E7	E7	E7 ‖
	Take me to the river.

	E7 D A
Verse 3	I don't know why I love you like I do,
	E7 D A
	After all the things that you put me through.
	E7 D A
	The sixteen candles that burn on my wall
	E7 D
	Turning me into the biggest fool of them all.

	A C Csus4 C Csus4
Pre-chorus 3	I wanna know,
	C G Gsus4 G Gsus4 G
	Baby tell me, _____
	D Dsus4 D Dsus4 D A7
	Am I in ____ love ____ to stay? Hey, hey, hey.

	E7
Outro	I wanna know, take me to the river.
	I wanna know, I want you to dip me in the water.
	I wanna know,
	‖: Wash me in the water. :‖ *Repeat to fade*

Try A Little Tenderness

Words & Music by
Harry Woods, Jimmy Campbell & Reg Connelly

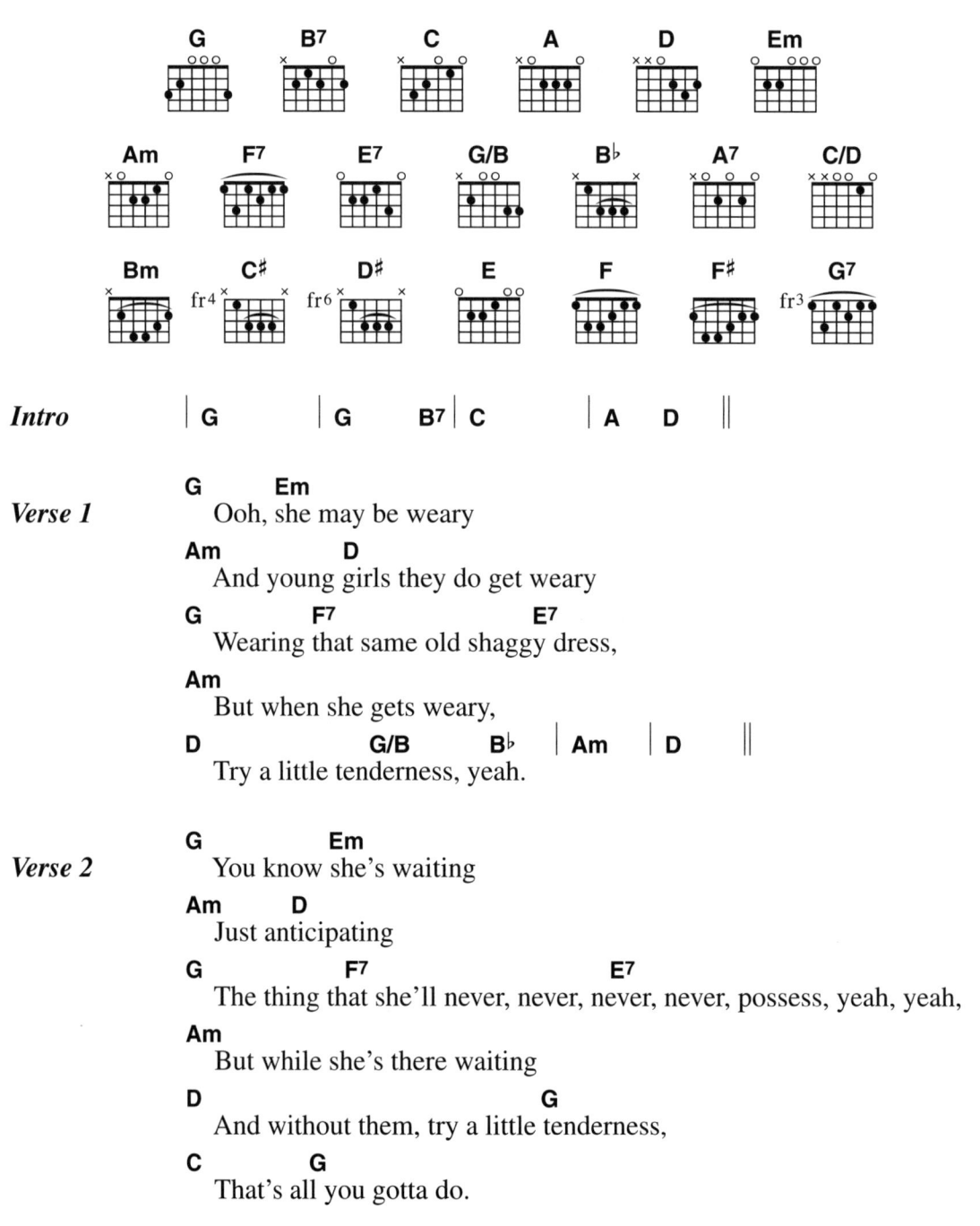

G   B7   C   A   D   Em
Am   F7   E7   G/B   B♭   A7   C/D
Bm   C♯   D♯   E   F   F♯   G7

Intro | G | G   B7 | C | A   D ||

Verse 1
G   Em
Ooh, she may be weary
Am   D
And young girls they do get weary
G   F7   E7
Wearing that same old shaggy dress,
Am
But when she gets weary,
D   G/B   B♭ | Am | D ||
Try a little tenderness, yeah.

Verse 2
G   Em
You know she's waiting
Am   D
Just anticipating
G   F7   E7
The thing that she'll never, never, never, never, possess, yeah, yeah,
Am
But while she's there waiting
D   G
And without them, try a little tenderness,
C   G
That's all you gotta do.

© Copyright 1932 & 1960 Campbell Connelly & Company Limited, 8/9 Frith Street, London W1.
All Rights Reserved. International Copyright Secured.

Bridge

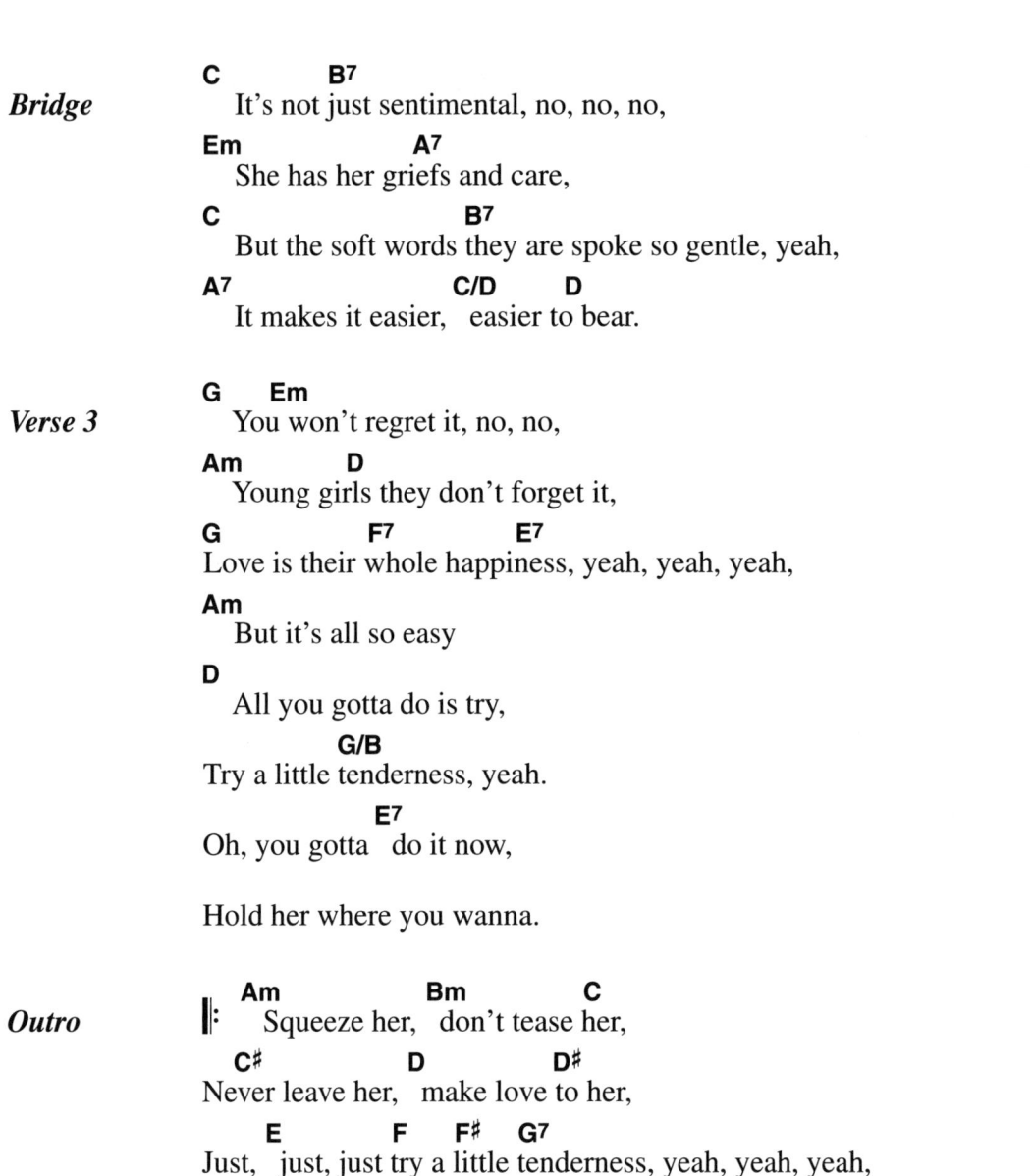

      C   **B7**
It's not just sentimental, no, no, no,
Em   **A7**
She has her griefs and care,
C   **B7**
But the soft words they are spoke so gentle, yeah,
A7   **C/D**   **D**
It makes it easier,   easier to bear.

Verse 3

  G   **Em**
You won't regret it, no, no,
Am   **D**
Young girls they don't forget it,
G   **F7**   **E7**
Love is their whole happiness, yeah, yeah, yeah,
Am
But it's all so easy
D
All you gotta do is try,
           G/B
Try a little tenderness, yeah.
           E7
Oh, you gotta   do it now,

Hold her where you wanna.

Outro

||: **Am**   **Bm**   **C**
Squeeze her,   don't tease her,
  C♯   **D**   **D♯**
Never leave her,   make love to her,
    E   **F** **F♯** **G7**
Just, just, just try a little tenderness, yeah, yeah, yeah,
F7   **E7**
You've gotta know how to love her, man. :|| *Repeat to fade*
                                               with vocal ad lib.

Under The Boardwalk

Words & Music by
Art Resnick & Kenny Young

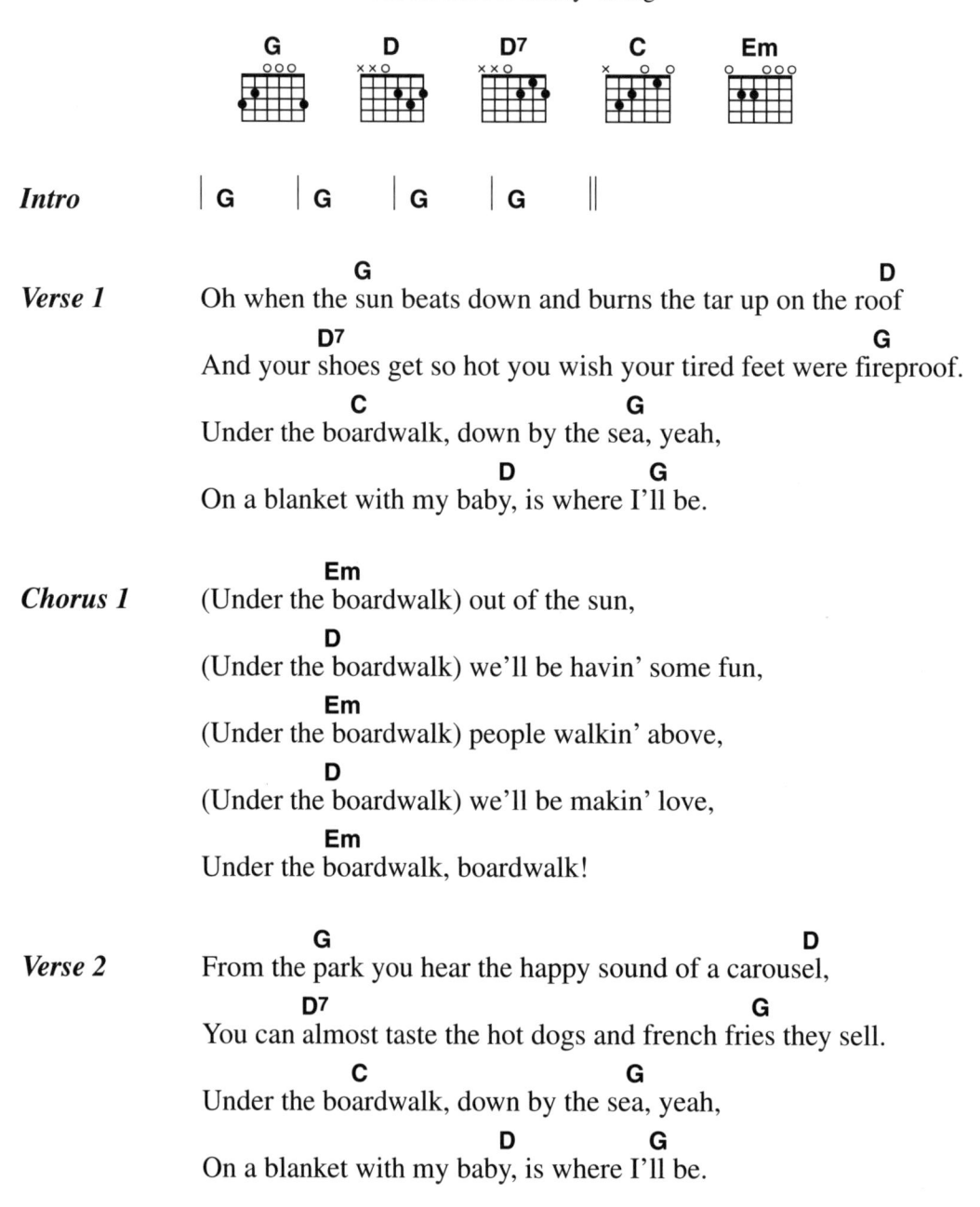

G   D   D7   C   Em

Intro | G | G | G | G ‖

Verse 1
           G   D
Oh when the sun beats down and burns the tar up on the roof
    D7   G
And your shoes get so hot you wish your tired feet were fireproof.
                 C   G
Under the boardwalk, down by the sea, yeah,
                         D   G
On a blanket with my baby, is where I'll be.

Chorus 1
           Em
(Under the boardwalk) out of the sun,
           D
(Under the boardwalk) we'll be havin' some fun,
           Em
(Under the boardwalk) people walkin' above,
           D
(Under the boardwalk) we'll be makin' love,
           Em
Under the boardwalk, boardwalk!

Verse 2
         G   D
From the park you hear the happy sound of a carousel,
   D7   G
You can almost taste the hot dogs and french fries they sell.
                 C   G
Under the boardwalk, down by the sea, yeah,
                         D   G
On a blanket with my baby, is where I'll be.

© Copyright 1964 T.M. Music Incorporated, New York, USA.
T.M. Music Limited, Iron Bridge House, 3 Bridge Approach, London NW1 for the British Commonwealth
(excluding Canada and Australasia) and the Republic of Ireland.
All Rights Reserved. International Copyright Secured.

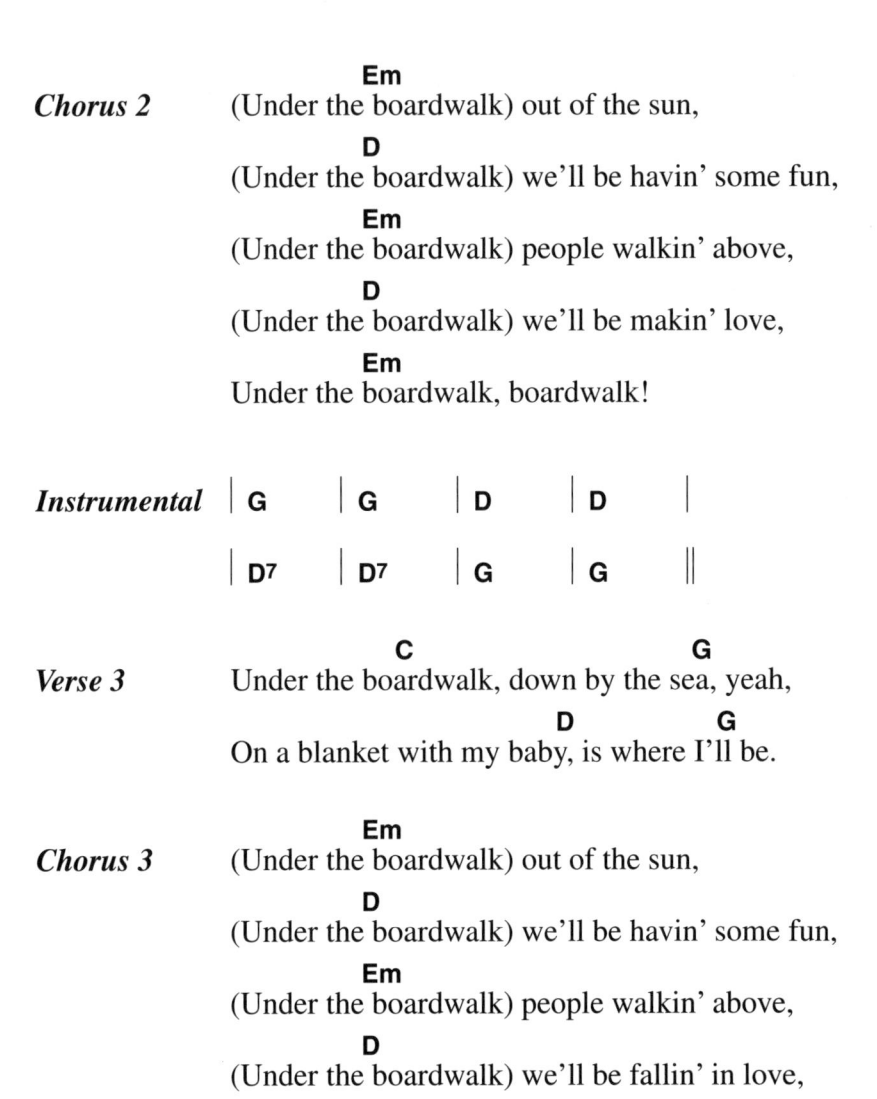

Chorus 2
          Em
(Under the boardwalk) out of the sun,
         D
(Under the boardwalk) we'll be havin' some fun,
         Em
(Under the boardwalk) people walkin' above,
         D
(Under the boardwalk) we'll be makin' love,
         Em
Under the boardwalk, boardwalk!

Instrumental | **G** | **G** | **D** | **D** |
                  | **D7** | **D7** | **G** | **G** ||

Verse 3
        C   **G**
Under the boardwalk, down by the sea, yeah,
                   D   **G**
On a blanket with my baby, is where I'll be.

Chorus 3
          Em
(Under the boardwalk) out of the sun,
         D
(Under the boardwalk) we'll be havin' some fun,
         Em
(Under the boardwalk) people walkin' above,
         D
(Under the boardwalk) we'll be fallin' in love,
         Em
Under the boardwalk, boardwalk!

What'd I Say

Words & Music by
Ray Charles

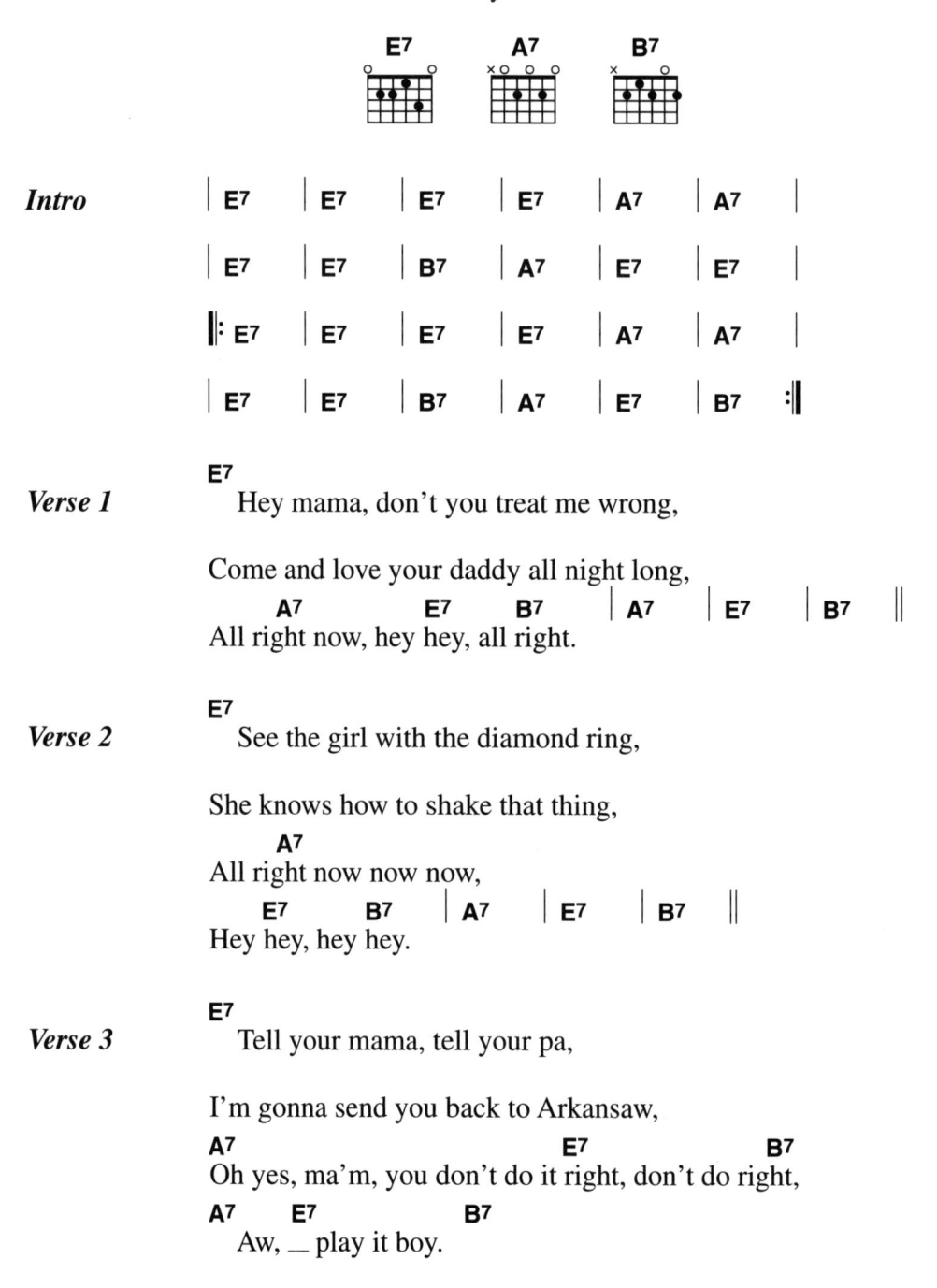

E7   A7   B7

Intro

| E7 | E7 | E7 | E7 | A7 | A7 |

| E7 | E7 | B7 | A7 | E7 | E7 |

‖: E7 | E7 | E7 | E7 | A7 | A7 |

| E7 | E7 | B7 | A7 | E7 | B7 :‖

Verse 1

    E7
Hey mama, don't you treat me wrong,

Come and love your daddy all night long,
  A7   E7   B7 | A7 | E7 | B7 ‖
All right now, hey hey, all right.

Verse 2

    E7
See the girl with the diamond ring,

She knows how to shake that thing,
  A7
All right now now now,
  E7   B7 | A7 | E7 | B7 ‖
Hey hey, hey hey.

Verse 3

    E7
Tell your mama, tell your pa,

I'm gonna send you back to Arkansaw,
A7   E7   B7
Oh yes, ma'm, you don't do it right, don't do right,
A7 E7   B7
Aw, _ play it boy.

© Copyright 1959 & 1961 Hill & Range Songs Incorporated, USA.
Carlin Music Corporation, Iron Bridge House, 3 Bridge Approach, London NW1.
All Rights Reserved. International Copyright Secured.

		E7	E7	E7	E7	A7	A7	
Instrumental								
		E7	E7	B7	A7	E7	B7	‖

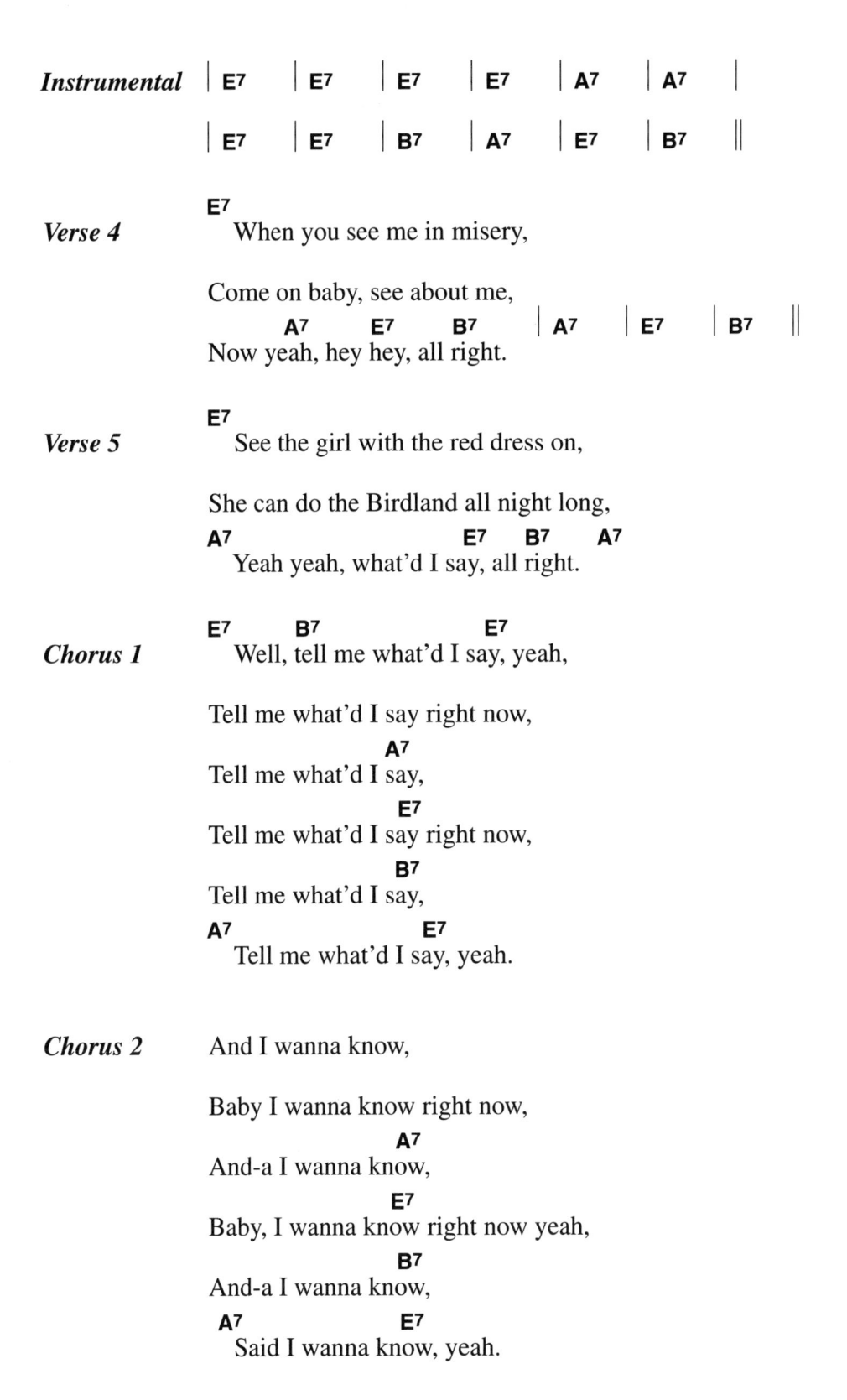

Verse 4

    E7
When you see me in misery,

Come on baby, see about me,
      A7   E7   B7 | A7 | E7 | B7   ‖
Now yeah, hey hey, all right.

Verse 5

    E7
See the girl with the red dress on,

She can do the Birdland all night long,
A7   E7   B7   A7
   Yeah yeah, what'd I say, all right.

Chorus 1

E7   B7   E7
   Well, tell me what'd I say, yeah,

Tell me what'd I say right now,
          A7
Tell me what'd I say,
          E7
Tell me what'd I say right now,
          B7
Tell me what'd I say,
A7   E7
   Tell me what'd I say, yeah.

Chorus 2

And I wanna know,

Baby I wanna know right now,
        A7
And-a I wanna know,
        E7
Baby, I wanna know right now yeah,
        B7
And-a I wanna know,
 A7   E7
  Said I wanna know, yeah.

Why Can't We Live Together

Words & Music by
Timmy Thomas

Gmaj7   F#m7   A   B   Bm

Intro | Drums for five bars ||

‖: Gmaj7 | Gmaj7 | F#m7 | F#m7 :‖ A | A | B | B |

‖: Gmaj7 | Gmaj7 | F#m7 | F#m7 :‖ A | A | B | B |

‖: (B) | (B) | (B) | (B) :‖ Gmaj7 | Gmaj7 | F#m7 | F#m7 ‖

Verse 1

Gmaj7
Tell me why, tell me why, tell me why,
F#m7
Umm, why can't we live together?
Gmaj7
Tell me why, tell me why,
F#m7
Umm, why can't we live together?
A
Everybody wants to live together,
B
Why can't we live together?

Verse 2

Gmaj7
No more wars, no more wars, no more wars,
F#m7
Umm, just a little peace in this world.
Gmaj7
No more wars, no more wars,
F#m7
All we want is some peace in this world.

© Copyright 1972 Sherlyn Publishing Company Incorporated, USA.
Peermusic (UK) Limited, 8-14 Verulam Street, London WC1.
All Rights Reserved. International Copyright Secured.

cont.

  A
   Everybody wants to live together,
   B
Why can't we live together?

Bridge

  (B)
   Gotta live, gotta live,

Gotta live together,

Gotta live together.

Verse 3

  Gmaj7
   No matter, no matter what colour,
  F♯m7
Umm, you are still my brother.
   Gmaj7
I said no matter, no matter what colour,
  F♯m7
Umm, you are still my brother.
 A
  Everybody wants to live together,
  B
Why can't we live together?

Outro solo   ‖: **Bm** | **Bm** | **Bm** | **Bm** :‖   *Repeat to fade*

Relative Tuning

The guitar can be tuned with the aid of pitch pipes or dedicated electronic guitar tuners which are available through your local music dealer. If you do not have a tuning device, you can use relative tuning. Estimate the pitch of the 6th string as near as possible to E or at least a comfortable pitch (not too high, as you might break other strings in tuning up). Then, while checking the various positions on the diagram, place a finger from your left hand on the:

5th fret of the E or 6th string and **tune the open A** (or 5th string) to the note (A)

5th fret of the A or 5th string and **tune the open D** (or 4th string) to the note (D)

5th fret of the D or 4th string and **tune the open G** (or 3rd string) to the note (G)

4th fret of the G or 3rd string and **tune the open B** (or 2nd string) to the note (B)

5th fret of the B or 2nd string and **tune the open E** (or 1st string) to the note (E)

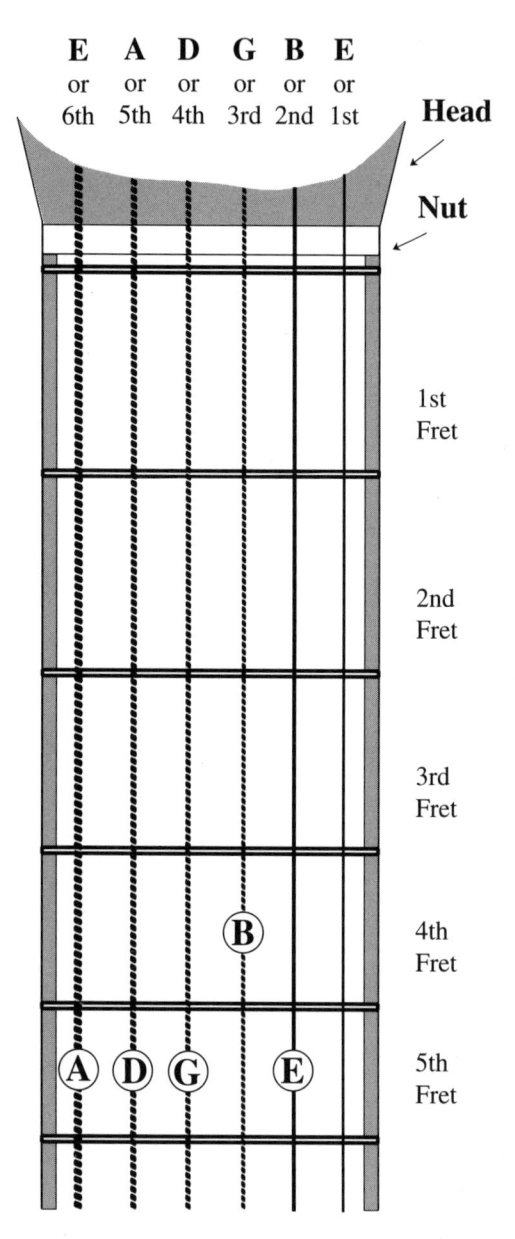

Reading Chord Boxes

Chord boxes are diagrams of the guitar neck viewed head upwards, face on as illustrated. The top horizontal line is the nut, unless a higher fret number is indicated, the others are the frets.

The vertical lines are the strings, starting from E (or 6th) on the left to E (or 1st) on the right.

The black dots indicate where to place your fingers.

Strings marked with an O are played open, not fretted.

Strings marked with an X should not be played.

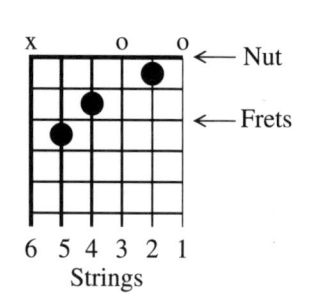